All Your Prayers
are Answered

All Your Prayers are Answered

Sam Menahem Ph.D.

Writer's Showcase
presented by *Writer's Digest*
San Jose New York Lincoln Shanghai

All Your Prayers are Answered

Writer's Showcase
presented by *Writer's Digest*
an imprint of iUniverse.com, Inc.

For information address:
iUniverse.com, Inc.
620 North 48th Street, Suite 201
Lincoln, NE 68504-3467
www.iuniverse.com

ISBN: 0-595-13002-X

Printed in the United States of America

This book is dedicated to my wife, Susan and my daughter,

Lauren who are the answers to my prayers.

CONTENTS

ACKNOWLEDGEMENTS

It takes many people to make a book. I would like to thank my editor, Phyllis Butler, my technical assistant Martin Rosch, my friends Barry Farber, Seymour Boorstein, my mother Anne Menahem, Alan Fortier, and Joyce Fischback for reading the manuscript and making helpful comments. I would also like to thank my friends Art Joseph, Marcy Prisco, Michael Grosso, Louise Northcutt, and Ed Hoffman and my brother, Lew Menahem, for their encouragement and support. Finally I would like to thank my wife Susan and daughter Lauren for their love which they share with me daily.

INTRODUCTION

Beyond Therapy

Several years ago a patient tried to kill me. Amazingly, this attack was the answer to my prayers. How could an assault be the answer to a prayer?

This patient, a large burly woman, was very unhappy with her life. When her life didn't improve with therapy, she also became frustrated and angry. I tried very hard to help, to no avail. I consulted colleagues and supervisors-the situation didn't improve. I began to feel as bad as she did and it seemed like no one could help me help her. Suddenly, the solution hit me, only God could help. I had to pray. But what should I pray for? I had little experience with prayer. I was brought up Jewish, but more in terms of spirituality than practice in prayer. My father once said he couldn't move his little pinky without God. I agreed with my father's feeling about the power of God. So, maybe God could help me now. I followed my intuition and prayed to be released from the situation. As I prayed, I also listened, and became aware of a repetitive thought, "It will soon end, in an unusual way." I wondered if this was wishful thinking or an answer from a higher source.

One day, the woman was particularly distraught, angry and unhappy. She began to verbally lambaste me. Then, without warning, she pulled a knife out of her coat and lunged at me, knocking me down. I struggled to get a hand free. Suddenly, something came over me and instead of struggling, I called out to her, "calm down, now; calm down." Miraculously, she let go of me and began to sob. Of course, she didn't really mean to hurt me. She had told me many times that I had saved her life…she was just frustrated and didn't know what to do. This all occurred on the eve of Passover, the Jewish holiday of freedom. On the eve of this holiday, my prayers *surely were* answered in an unusual way. Both my patient and I were freed from the therapeutic impasse. And our lives were changed forever.

Are all prayers answered? For those who are strong believers in God this is a given. However, for many others, though they want to believe that their prayers are answered, "common sense" leads them to doubt this assertion. How could a loving God allow the holocaust or Bosnia's "ethnic cleansing" to take place? What about AIDs and cancer? Many sick people pray and are prayed for, yet they suffer and die young. People who want to believe in the power of prayer frequently pray during times of illness, deprivation and death in the family. Sometimes their prayers seem to be answered, often not. How can we understand this? What are we to believe?

Whether prayers are answered or not, most of us continue to pray. Polls show that 90 % of Americans prayed in 1957 and 90% of Americans pray today. Obviously, most people in this country retain some belief in the efficacy of prayer, but why are the results so confusing? Perhaps we don't understand our relationship to God. When we realize that at some level we are God, we pray differently.

When prayer doesn't seem to work we have varying reactions. Some people begin to doubt that there is a God, while others feel that there must be something wrong with *them*. Perhaps, they think, there is a God, but they are unworthy of having their prayers answered because of some perceived bad behavior. Perhaps they are praying incorrectly; maybe prayers are answered only selectively. Could it be that prayer doesn't really work at all in the physical world. Or is it that God is too busy to answer the prayers of every little person? In his book, *When Bad Things Happen To Good People,* Rabbi Harold Kushner suggests that perhaps God is powerful but not omnipotent. Omnipotence implies that God can intervene in human affairs at any time and change the course of events. If bad things happen, God is choosing not to get involved. Instead of having the power to change things, Rabbi Kushner suggests that God's power lies in inspiring us to develop compassion and love for ourselves and each other despite the troubles we go through. I agree with the Rabbi but this is only a partial answer.

This book will present a spiritual viewpoint that incorporates inspiration by an omnipotence of God. God has varying reactions to prayer. Sometimes God does inspire us to love more; sometimes we are helped by amazing coincidences; sometimes the answer to our prayers is "no", and sometimes miracles do happen. This book suggests that there are reasons for each of God's responses to prayer. These reasons will lead us to more effective prayer and more fulfilling lives.

In my first book, *When Therapy Isn't Enough: The Healing Power Of Prayer and Psychotherapy*, I set forth a psychological/spiritual model of life. My hypothesis was that prayer could help therapy and therapy could help prayer. This model, based on the work of developmental psychologists and transpersonal theorist Ken Wilber among others, posits that life follows an orderly developmental sequence. The psychologists explain how we grow up from self centered little toddlers, through the identity crises of adolescence and the existential crises of middle adulthood. This is the psychological growth process. It involves maturing by resolving the hurts of our individual psyches. The theory states that we often get stuck at early stages of development due to the traumatic events of our life. This "stuckness", say the developmental theorists, accounts for our psychological problems in later life.

Transpersonal psychologists carry the theory further. They tell us that our "arrested development" leads us to forget that we are spiritual beings, so we place all our faith in a more limited "egoic" or self-centered consciousness. From this point of view, we are primarily physical creatures, directed by a psychological ego. We are separate, fragile beings, dealing with a difficult world. Having been hurt already in childhood, we must defend ourselves against further wounds by others at all costs. Early traumas and hurt feelings have convinced us that we are alone and isolated in a dangerous world. Psychologists urge us to transcend the childhood traumas through psychotherapy. The hope is that as we explore, re-experience and let go of the old hurts, we will develop a stronger so called ego that will then help us cope better with the perceived harsh outside world. It never occurs to mainstream psychologists that peace can only be attained by allying the strengthened ego with the spiritual or Higher Self. Most psychologists don't believe in a Higher Self.

There are therapists and spiritual theorists with other points of view, however, that do recognize the importance of this spiritual alliance in leading a peaceful, happy life. Eastern Religions such as Buddhism and Vedanta Hinduism and transpersonal theories presented by Wilber, Jung, Assagioli and Washburn for example, suggest that we progress through several more stages of growth beyond the psychological, which are essentially spiritual in nature, and can be developed through interaction with spirit via prayer and meditation. As we go through the prayer/meditation, healing process, we become more loving, mature, secure and interested in serving others. It is in this service that we find meaning, transcending selfish goals and doing what we feel guided to do, helping us toward ultimate enlightenment (sometimes called satori or nirvana by Buddhists or Hindus). This is the complete freedom from all emotional, mental or psychic tension. The alliance of ego and Spirit via prayer and meditation moves us in this direction.

As we progress on this path toward peace, life becomes more and more a process wherein the struggles and difficulties are seen as opportunities for further spiritual progress. This doesn't mean that nothing painful ever happens to us. It means that we look at the pain differently, from the perspective of the Higher Self. What once seemed like pure psychological problems now take on a spiritual hue. It begins to occur to many of us that the answers to life's basic psychological problems are spiritual. Fear is healed by faith. Guilt is resolved by forgiveness. Inferiority yields to strength. Hate is cured by love. Prayer is an essential tool to apply these spiritual antidotes to the "normal" problems of living.

We realize gradually, that our problems are actually caused by our stubborn insistence that we are primarily separate, physical creatures in a competitive struggle for survival. We have tried to replace Spirit with ego and it doesn't work. Spirit is our source. All of our religious traditions tell us this spirit, often called God, is a never ending source of love and sustenance. Our ego is a temporary structure, developed over time to help us deal with the world. The separation-individuation process results in our feeling that this conscious ego is in charge. Mainstream psychology agrees and in fact tells us to strengthen the conscious ego in time of stress. Unfortunately, psychologists don't tell us that the strengthened ego often forgets its spiritual source and tries to convince each of us that we are nothing but a body directed by our ego. This results in a never-ending system of defenses which are well documented by Sigmund Freud, Anna Freud and many others.

At best, the strong ego is a well defended fortress with intense underlying fears. At worst, the weak ego, overwhelmed by fear and guilt, flounders around looking for help in what seems to be a battle with a hostile world. If we have a weak ego (sometimes called low self esteem), we may turn to drugs, more powerful people, therapists or religion. Even if we pray, what we are often looking for is help from a powerful outside God to bail us out. This kind of prayer, practiced from the ego's point of view, is a mistake, as it reinforces the idea that we are separate and weak. It is one of the factors which makes us sometimes doubt the efficacy of prayer. But at least we are going in a direction which may eventually help us. It will help the most when we learn to pray from the point of view of the Higher Self.

Prayer is a dynamic interaction with the unseen spiritual world, which is deeper and wider than the personal, Freudian unconscious. Psychological growth theory sees the personal unconscious as a hotbed of repressed traumas, sexual and aggressive drives. The ego is seen as a mediator between these strong drives. Strengthening this ego is seen as the only way to referee in the battle between the unconscious "id" (sex, aggression) and the "superego" (conscience). Strengthening the ego, however, is helpful only in a very limited sense. A structured, stronger sense of Self can develop the humility to later ally with the Higher Self and truly heal the soul.

Spiritual psychological theory recognizes the existence in the unconscious of the conflicts, traumas, drives and distorted thinking. But spiritual psychology sees *much more* in the unconscious; it includes a spiritual source of being. Thus, there is more to healing than just strengthening the mediating ego because the unconscious is personal *and transpersonal*. This means that, in addition to the personal unconscious self, with all its conflicts, there is also a Higher Spiritual Self, which is connected to God, however he/she is understood, and has *no conflict*. Transpersonal theory suggests that this wider conception of the unconscious opens the possibility of true healing and happiness, because it leads us beyond fear, guilt, hate and inferiority. Psychological ego strengthening is a temporary measure, which can lead to a healing alliance with the Spiritual Self. The ego can never really be secure, but with a lessening of conflict it may become flexible enough to try another approach to gnawing problems. By mid-life, spiritual hunger often grows. This is the Higher Self calling for a return to Spirit, with its emphasis on love, forgiveness, faith, and strength which are the natural outgrowths of knowledge of the unity of all things.

Prayer is the missing link between psychology and spirituality, between mere ego strengthening and soul healing. Prayer helps us to see that the ego needs to *join with the Higher Self for healing to take place.* This is the *healing alliance.* Prayer can help us see that inner peace can only come when life is seen from the spiritual framework of beliefs. The spiritual belief system tells us to cooperate with the life process. It teaches us something we need to know in order to lead peaceful lives, *spiritual consciousness underlies physical reality.* Our mistaken belief that we are merely separate bodies driven by ego consciousness leads us to lives defending ourselves against fear and guilt.

In this book, I will explore the ways in which prayer and meditation work, how to pray effectively and how to recognize the answers to our prayers. I will explore the evidence for the importance of a shift from the egoic to the spiritual point of view, and the probable outcomes of this spiritual cognitive shift in our way of thinking. This is a mighty task, but my own spiritual guidance says it is time to begin the synthesis which will provide the tools for true healing.

This book is a synthesis of developmental psychology, cognitive psychology, self psychology, transpersonal psychology, metaphysics, mysticism, kabbalistic Judaism, esoteric Christianity, New Thought philosophy, Buddhism, Vedantic Hinduism and more. I will be explaining, in plain language, why all prayers are answered and what to do to get your life to be more of a meaningful growth process and less of a pointless suffering process. Life is a struggle. *It is supposed to be that way, until we wake up to basic spiritual truth, all minds are joined in God and the nature of God is love.* This insight will change our lives.

This book is written from the point of view that the key to life is *to use* our lives, as *well as* we can, to love as many people as we can (including ourselves), as often as we can. Prayer when practiced diligently from the heart, can be an invaluable part of the growth process. Life is already a prayer, but it is a misdirected prayer. We are praying from the narrow, limited view of the ego. We are praying to be protected from our fear and guilt. As soon as we wake up and realize how to pray from the point of view of the Higher Self, our lives will be transformed into expressions of love for all sentient beings. I hope this book will be an aid in your awakening process. Let us begin.

CHAPTER ONE

WE PRAY MORE THAN WE THINK WE DO

Prayer is usually thought of as a ritual, a reverent petition to a Higher Power. We feel scared or helpless and we ask for something we lack, that something is control. Our prayers are usually a plea to fulfill a need for safety, material goods, healing or love. Note that we are *pleading* with some powerful force *outside ourselves* to help us. We are scared because we see ourselves as weak, lacking, and often unworthy. We think we are nothing but separate bodies, directed by egos. We may add to our petitions reasons why our prayers should be answered. Then we wait. If the healing (usually physical), money or romance doesn't appear soon, we decide that prayer just doesn't work. In other words, prayer isn't magic and it's magic we're looking for. When our prayers don't work, we may blame ourselves, others, or God. Even so, we are reluctant to give up our Santa Claus theory of God. If we are good, Santa (God) will give us whatever we want, we just have to ask for it.

There are reasons why that Santa Claus world doesn't exist. Think of the implications of a world where each person's whims were swiftly granted. Imagine the chaos that kind of world would create. Some people might be prudent and only ask for what they need while others might stockpile wealth, seek to hurt their enemies and over-power their neighbors. Surely no one would ever die. At the first sign of illness, we would just pray and be healed immediately. What would happen when two or more individual's wishes were in

1

conflict? It is difficult to imagine anything but chaos. Only in a world of wise, loving, mature, peaceful people could every prayer be answered directly and immediately without any effort on the part of the petitioner.

So then, perhaps the reason prayer is answered indirectly is that humankind is not yet ready for immediate answers. First, we all need to become wiser, more loving, more mature and more peaceful. In fact, it could be that the world is set up so that we can (if we choose to) learn through our life process how to become more wise, loving, mature and peaceful. Let us examine this idea further, using health problems as an example.

Prayer and Health

Most health problems are the result of stress, poor diet, environmental problems, genetic factors, infectious agents and karmic factors. In the Santa Claus world, we could get totally stressed out, eat only Twinkies, drink beer, pollute our food and water supply and sneeze in each other's face. As soon as we felt ill, we could just pray to Santa God to restore our perfect health and he would. We would, of course, learn nothing. We would destroy the environment and violate every law of nature (especially the law of cause and effect). Yet, Santa God would just keep bailing us out at every request. This sounds remarkably like the situation with a spoiled child. The indulged child always gets bailed out and never learns how to get along with anyone or how to operate within the law of cause and effect. We pity such children. Imagine a world where everyone is a spoiled brat.

I don't think that's what the *real* God wants. The world is not ordered that way. God has laws, like the law of cause and effect. As each person learns the laws of the world, he thinks, feels and behaves with these laws in mind. A large part of maturity is learning to accept the law of cause and effect (sometimes called karma), thereby setting in motion positive thoughts, feelings and behaviors, which *tend* to cause positive outcomes. Emotionally well balanced, well nourished, community minded, giving, loving people *tend* to be much healthier than stressed out, angry, resentful, anxious misanthropes. The former are operating out of their Higher Self. The latter are operating out of their ego.

Notice I use the word, "tend." I am vastly oversimplifying the process of creating health or illness. Health is a complex interaction of thoughts, feelings, genetics, karma, environment, behavior, bacteria and viruses. Most illnesses are caused by two or more of these factors. What purpose could be served if the return to health were as simple as mumbling a quick prayer to reverse all the negative factors that caused the illness in the first place. We get sick because we are unaware of the potential health problems we are causing by negative thinking, feeling, behaving and destruction of the environment. We are unaware of the health costs of ignoring the Higher Self in favor of the ego.

We are often amazed when we become ill because we are ignorant of the relentless, slow process of creating the illness. We only become aware that something is wrong when we have pain or disability. Sometimes, it is too late to reverse the physical illness, but if we can become aware of the slow process of forming the illness, we can begin the often equally slow process of healing it. This lack of awareness is the situation of most people. We are unaware of our responsibility in causing the illness and want a quick, no effort cure from the doctor, medicine or even God through prayer. It just doesn't work that way, it shouldn't. As spiritual healer Joel Goldsmith states, the true healing is of the soul anyway and it is never too late to heal the soul. Actually, the soul is already healed because it is pure spirit. Recognition of this perfection is what we call the healing. We call it a healing when the body seems cured but peace of mind, maturity, and lovingkindness are also indicators of healing; spiritual healing.

It would be fascinating if we could get a computer print out of all our thoughts, conscious and unconscious, as well as our feelings for one day, then correlate this printout with our health. I think most of us would be amazed at how judgmental and negative we are. If we could realize what we were thinking, we might have an easier time seeing the connections between thoughts, feelings and health. There is also a connection between our spiritual health and physical health but it is not perfectly causal. Goldsmith tells us at the spiritual level healing can take place instantaneously, as there is no cause and effect. This may or may not result in a physical cure, but it is what Goldsmith calls the "click" that is most important. Such concepts and his method of prayer will be discussed in more detail in a later chapter.

Prayer and Wealth

Let us look at the connection between prayer and wealth. It is interesting to me how many people play the lottery and even pray to win the big prize. Despite the tremendous odds against them, people pay money for a chance at an easy life with no effort. They hope that by luck or chance they will soon live on easy street, in luxury, with no need to work any more. It must seem like a magical answer to the unhappiness of their lives. It also must be very disappointing when they don't win.

Many people who do win the big prize are surprised to find it does not answer all their problems as they thought it would. Instead, new problems are created. They are besieged by people who want to invest or to steal their money. Relatives ask for gifts and loans. How should they allocate the money? Do they really have enough to fulfill their dreams and is life still meaningful without the daily process of earning a living? Now they may be bored. The adjustments are endless. Perhaps money isn't the answer. Research shows that after one year, lottery winners are not much happier than the general population.

Again, imagine a world in which prayer was directly answered as if by magic. Wouldn't everyone win the lottery? How could that be? Huge jackpots would be split so many ways they would be minuscule, canceling the whole process. Even if *everyone* could win the lottery and be materially wealthy with no effort, where would that leave the world. Would most people still want to work? Would menial jobs get done? What would people do with their time? Obviously, the world was not meant to be populated by bored, lazy lottery winners. I believe part of God's plan is for each person to do something meaningful with their lives. Working for a living is usually part of the equation. Does that mean prayers aren't answered? Or does it mean that prayer works in ways other than direct supernatural solutions?

Prayer and Romantic Love

Let us look at the relationship between prayer and romantic love. Imagine a world in which any prayer for *a particular person to love us* was answered. Lillian Lonely prays for Studley Megabucks to love her and he does. But what about the other million women who pray for a Studley Megabucks? And what about Studley-does he have any say in the matter? Clearly this type of magical prayer could not work in matters of the heart. There has to be mutual choice and attraction. We are attracted to people who will help us work out our psychological and even spiritual issues.

That doesn't mean we can't create a *general* prayer for someone to love us! Prayer can help us find love in this more indirect way. I had one patient who prayed for love. Her prayer was: "Thank you God for sending me a man who is good for me, and whom I will marry." She met and married such a man within a year, after diligently applying this heartfelt affirmative prayer. The prayer was not direct, as she did not specify the exact person she wanted. In fact, the man she married was quite different from her usual type. They have now been happily married for many years.

Tuning into God's Will

Life is much too complex for all prayers to be *directly* answered at the whim of each person. We must look deeper than our conscious ego-centered desires to have a better life. There is a deeper part of us all. Psychiatrist Roberto Assagioli called it the superconscious. By opening up to superconscious guidance, we are in effect following God's will. It is vitally important to realize that our unconscious is made up of *much more* than repressed memories and sexual urges. We are connected to God through the superconscious and need to realize this to be helped. When we open to God's guidance, we may pray more effectively and recognize the answers. When we widen our definition of prayer, seeing it as a spiritual-psychological creative process, life is more understandable.

Thoughts Are Things: Prayers Are Thoughts

Most prayer is cognitive, in that it is composed of thoughts or spoken words, powered by feelings. This is true for three of the four types of prayer: petition, intercession and adoration. In each of these types of prayers we ask God for something or affirm some aspect of God. We use thoughts and words. Both the Buddhists and "new thought" philosophies (e.g. Unity, Science of Mind) tell us that "thoughts are things." Specifically, they are electromagnetic waves or particles. Perhaps, in measuring our brain waves by means of an EEG (electroencephalogram) test, we are measuring thought patterns as well. We know that we can train ourselves to produce more alpha waves (relaxed) via biofeedback. The biofeedback equipment tells us when we are creating a relaxed thought pattern by signaling with a noise.

If we spend too much time producing distressing brain waves (too many negative thoughts), we may cause injury to the body by producing too many stress related hormones. There is an entire new branch of medicine, psychoneuroimmunology (PNI), that is concerned with *how* thoughts and feelings effect the immune system. For example, adrenaline, a hormone, gives us energy to fight or flee. If we pump adrenaline and don't fight or flee our body becomes stressed. Over a long period of time, our immune system may weaken due to stress and we may get sick with a virus, bacterial infection or other ailment. Our thoughts, powered by emotions, will have indirectly caused an illness through overproduction and misuse of hormones.

The same type of process occurs with psychological or interpersonal dysfunction. Fearful thoughts generate anxiety which is an aroused bodily state. We feel a need to run or fight without knowing why. So we don't run or fight, but continue to feel anxious. The anxiety then interferes with our social relationships and we begin to get down on ourselves, maybe even to the point of depression. Thus, thoughts can create all kinds of problems for us. If low level depression (the blues) is not treated, it may become clinical depression including feelings of despondency, worthlessness and failure on all levels. Depression can spread from the mind to the body.

In *The Nature of Personal Reality*, Jane Roberts tells us that "experience is the product of the mind, the spirit, conscious thoughts and feelings and unconscious thoughts and feelings." (p. xviii) In other words, thoughts, powered by feelings create our lives. It is important not to take this popular new age belief simplistically or literally. I must re-emphasize that this "creation of your own reality" is a long term *process* as I have briefly outlined above. Thus, you don't directly give yourself cancer by thinking negatively. But cancer can be one result of a long process initiated by thought. Hence, curing cancer is not simple either.

There are usually many factors involved in illness including thoughts, feelings, attitudes, diet, environment, genetics, viruses etc. The point here is that thoughts are things that (often indirectly) create our lives. We are thinking constantly, and our thoughts run the gamut from, "What should I eat for breakfast?" to "What is the nature of God?" But where do these thoughts "go?" Do they affect anything else? And what does all this have to do with prayer?

Are Prayers Directed Thoughts?

Since most prayer is made up of thoughts which are directed at God, what is the difference between prayers and our willy nilly thoughts? My feeling is that the main difference between prayers and thoughts is one of focus or directedness. My concept of God is a loving unity of all things. Prayers do not work because we send something to a superbeing who we imagine hears it and answers. Rather, I believe they are recorded on a sort of great cosmic videotape-called the "akashic records" by the great psychic and healer Edgar Cayce-ready to be processed and replayed as events in our lives. The metaphor is imperfect due to the symbolic and indirect nature of the playback but whatever prayers in the form of thoughts and feelings are produced will be manifested in some form. Our thoughts and feelings are affecting and creating our lives. They do so whether we call them prayers or not. All thoughts then, are very prayer like. In this way of thinking, our thoughts are prayers-whether they are directed or not-and are answered. The answers are our lives.

It is not only directed prayer thoughts that are recorded, played back and answered. *All* thoughts are produced and processed in this way. Thus, are our lives created. Though this is most clearly delineated in

Jane Roberts' material, it is also implied by ancient religions like Buddhism as well. "Right thinking" is part of the eightfold path of the Buddha. Buddhists recognize the importance of "right thinking" as part of the eightfold path to compassionate living. They recognize, however, that there is never perfect control. For Buddhists, it is not necessary to censor all negative thoughts, you merely become very aware but unattached to the thoughts, while following the eightfold path toward peace. The process of the eightfold path eventually leads to kinder, gentler, more compassionate living.

Undirected thought is informal prayer. Formal prayer, however, is an *intentionally* directed form of thought, designed to produce certain results, our personal idea of a better life. According to the American upwardly mobile or narcissistic school of thought, the direction should be fulfillment of our personal wishes and desires-success. According to religious tradition we should be aiming our prayers toward spiritual growth, trying to be better people. Hence the Judeo-Christian emphasis on study, prayer, and community service. This is comparable to the Buddhist concept of the eightfold path which includes right speech, right thought, right action, right livelihood, right aspiration, right understanding, right effort, right concentration and right mindfulness. Formal prayer is a way of directing thought towards higher purpose, meaning, peace and love between people. Thus, the direction, intensity and methods of prayer become important variables in creating both individual and group happiness and harmony. If we just let our willy nilly thoughts (non-directed prayers) be recorded and played back, our lives will be equally chaotic. If we pray for our personal desires to be fulfilled we run the risk of being too self centered and may miss the spiritual mark. If we pray for spiritual values, from the point of view of the Higher Self we become better people.

When people seek therapy, they are usually looking for *symptomatic* relief from depression, anxiety, guilt or relationship problems. The problem is not usually seen as embedded in their spiritual, psychological or social framework. Frequently, a good therapist can help them see the overall network of beliefs and what changes in their lives need to be made. In Ericksonian hypnosis we call this re-framing the problem. This requires looking at the situation from a different angle. For example, I often tell people that their anxiety is their best friend in that it points them toward the real problem: a deeply held negative belief that they are somehow in danger. An important part of healing is to place the problem within a new framework and look at its true source. Though medication can sometimes mask the symptom, it cannot heal the real source of the problem. I get the best results with people who are open to the most radical re-frame, the spiritual re-frame.

The shift here is from the ego and its quest for quick material pleasure and success to the Higher Self, with its desire for meaningful activity. This is a shift from victimization by a harsh and random environment to a life where events are looked at as meaningful coincidences that lead to insight and growth, peace and love. Sometimes this is called a paradigm shift.

The paradigm or world view is the lens through which we view our experiences. As we change our world view from material success to spiritual fulfillment our lives are transformed. In a world view guided by spiritual growth, we look for ways to develop compassion, forgiveness, meaning and inner peace. We look at our problems and symptoms as opportunities and challenges rather than obstacles to glory and entitlement. Our selfish, narcissistic goals change to compassionate, altruistic ones. We grow spiritually when we can see that our ego has deluded us into thinking we are separated from God and alone in a difficult world. As we learn to join with the Higher Self, the part of us connected to the divine, our symptoms fade and our relationships improve.

The 12 step programs have a saying, "you come for vanity and stay for sanity." Most people come to "Overeaters Anonymous" because they can't control their eating and often don't like the way they look. What they discover, if they "work the steps", is that there is more to life than looking good. Healing is much more than just symptom removal. When we recognize that there is a Higher Power that will help us when asked, we have taken a giant step toward true sanity. We may not know exactly what we want, but it has more to do with inner peace than getting more "stuff."

The Case of the Fearful Trader

A 47-year-old bond trader was referred to me by his physician for anxiety so debilitating that he could no longer work at his job on Wall Street. Steven, an Orthodox Jew, was deeply embarrassed about seeing a psychologist but he was desperate and a year of tranquilizers had not helped much. His story revealed a man addicted to material success. He had done very well at bond trading and was proud of himself. Through therapy, he realized he had wanted to succeed to compensate his mother for the loss of her elder son to cancer at the age of 11. The death was handled very poorly by both parents who allowed their surviving son to stay out of school six months after his brother's death, so no one would pity him.

After his brother's death, Steven took on a role like that of "JFK" (John Kennedy became president because his older brother Joe died in World War II). Likewise, Steven felt if his older brother couldn't achieve anything further in life, *he would.* Despite the stress of the "results" oriented, Wall Street environment, Steven did succeed beyond his wildest dreams. And he saw it as a triumph due to *his own* cleverness and talent. This kind of false pride often precedes a fall, and fall he did. First, the bond market went sour. He began to worry. His anxiety increased. Even though he broke-even in a bad market, he began to see himself as a failure, which led to more worry. He became so anxious, he could barely work. Then his mother died. The person he was trying to make happy through achievement was gone. He found he couldn't concentrate or work. He had to go on disability. He felt humiliated. He wanted to get back to work and continue his material success, but he couldn't. He believed the anxiety was merely circumstantial, not really related to his life. Perhaps the anxiety was a punishment from God. It was an illness his medical doctor couldn't cure.

Through the therapy process he began to see how *he* was unconsciously creating the anxiety through his thinking. His tremendous fear of failing at his work led to "what if..." thoughts which led to more anxiety. This sort of thinking is the same as unconsciously praying your way into a state of anxiety. Steven was so nervous he could no longer pursue his version of success.

I pointed out to him that "success" as he was defining it could be considered a form of idolatry. He was too absorbed in making a lot of money through his correct reading of the market. He was so afraid of making mistakes that he couldn't work. The Jewish religion suggests that God should come first in everyone's life. Study, prayer and good deeds are more important than material success. Thus, although Steven was orthodox, spirituality took a back seat to material success. He looked at any loss as a humiliating failure. Steven's idolatry crippled him because he forgot his priorities (according to his own religious tradition). Of course he lost confidence during the market slump. All he had to rely upon was his human self and he knew that he wasn't astute enough to be "infallible", nobody is. His ego could only accept perfection and God was unrelated to the picture. His goal was to get his confidence back and become infallible again. But he was too afraid of failure to try.

Although Steven prayed daily, it was not bringing him much comfort. His prayers were rote. He wanted God to fix his psychological problems by strengthening his ego. He continued to pray for magical removal of all anxiety so He could return to work with renewed confidence. This was his ego's plan. God's plan was different. I believed that he needed to cope with some anxiety and develop a new mind set.

Thus, I suggested a meditative prayer, repeating the word "shalom" as his mantra. He returned excitedly the next week to report that he had the most peaceful week in years. The "shalom" prayer was working. He was using shalom as a mantra. It temporarily took his mind away from his fears and this felt good.

Yet, thinking of work still made him anxious. He was still looking for magic. Instead I suggested that instead of hoping for magic, Steven use shalom as a reminder of the peace available when he chose God over his ego's desires. In other words he needed to choose faith that his needs were being taken care of. Each time he chose peace by meditating on shalom, he would be calmer. Once this became a habit, his spiritual values would give him a new kind of confidence and peace. Faith in a Higher Power is the antidote to fear. It is really the only true answer to anxiety disorders. He must learn to consistently choose peace.

Through prayer and therapy Steven is in the process of a true paradigm shift from valuing material success to spiritual growth. Choosing peace is God's plan for our salvation. When we consistently choose peace, our lives will unfold in ways that may surprise us but in the long run are in our best interest. The main point for Steven is not whether he ever makes a lot of money again. The point is that he realizes who or what is really in charge: God. Transpersonal theorist Michael Washburn tells us "When you surrender to the Ground of Being,...you are able to reintegrate, in service of transcendence." Steven is using prayer as a focus to turn his life creating process over to God. This is not avoiding responsibility as some people might claim. It is accepting that God provides the circumstances, we take the action. I do not know if his prayers will lead Steven back to Wall Street, but if he persists they will bring him into that mystical union that heals the soul at the deepest level. His life will become a prayer.

The Case of the Avoidant Lover

Hank was a forty seven year old gay man who came to therapy for depression due to his inability to enter into an intimate relationship. His feeling was that without such a relationship, life was no longer worth living. His history revealed that he had been despised and abused by his father and neglected by his narcissistic mother. His answer to this horrible treatment was to be a very good boy. He spent most of his time pleasing others and minimized his own needs.

As adolescence neared, his sexual needs emerged toward his own sex. Brief encounters with a neighborhood boy led to shame which he repressed. He forced himself to act as if he were heterosexual and even to marry. Eventually, however, he admitted to himself and others that he was homosexual and "came out." At first, sex was casual and anonymous, not unusual in the gay world. After a while when he had trouble developing true intimacy, he knew he needed help. He went for therapy and improved his life in many ways, but not with intimate relationships. This was the way he was when I met him: intelligent, warm, witty, well liked, successful in his career, *and* depressed.

Spirituality and prayer did not enter into our early discussions. He was not religious and did not really believe in God. He considered himself an agnostic, a scientist-an engineer. Early sessions focused on ways he might make advances toward men he liked. Nothing helped much and he tended to avoid any man he was attracted to. One day, he came in and stated that he was absolutely sure he should kill himself. Nothing I could say seemed to be able to sway him and *I* became anxious.

Suddenly, I remembered the most important thing, God. I silently prayed for guidance and determined I would follow that guidance. First, I was guided to invent an unusual hypnotic trance where I alternately touched his head on the left side and stated "shut up" and then the right side and stated "listen." I then hypnotically directed the intuitive unconscious part of him to think of all the reasons he had for living and to let time pass until the depression lifted.

My second intuition was much more traditional: get him on medication. Hank protested vehemently that medication would make him like his crazy sister. I reassured him and persisted until he finally agreed to see his friend, a physician, and be evaluated for anti-depressants. He promised not to kill himself, at least until he saw me again. As he left I told him I had prayed for guidance and asked if I could pray for him; he agreed.

This was his first turning point. Certainly the medication helped but so did his evolving "world view." He was able to see that he actually could be happy with or without an intimate friend. He became interested in spirituality and began to pray daily. He primarily used prayers of thankfulness for all that he had. Yet, the lack of an intimate relationship nagged at him.

Eventually, Hank became interested in Buddhism, and one day we were discussing the concept of enlightenment. I quoted Buddhist scholar Robert Thurman's question, "What is the point in not being enlightened?" This hit him like a thunderbolt. He understood that if he got enlightened, his life was O.K. any way it was. This was his second turning point. Paradoxically, it enabled him to better understand himself psychologically and work on himself. He saw the role shame played in his sexual difficulties.

Today, he no longer speaks of suicide and continues to work on this issue with a much lighter heart. His life is infinitely better than ever before. He has transformed his insistence on an intimate relationship or death into a quest for spiritual growth.

In both of these cases a radical transformation is in process. Steven describes himself as kinder, gentler, less controlling and in general, a calmer person. The insights of therapy have led him to a closer concordance with the truth of his orthodox Jewish beliefs. Instead of praying in a rote manner, he now prays from the heart for guidance, acceptance of self and increased faith. He may or may not return to Wall Street, but he will continue to shift his focus from narcissistic insistence on his work and financial desires being met to a God centered life.

Hank has also changed radically, from holding a strictly scientific, random world view, to creating his own reality within a spiritual universe. He now works hard at changing what he can change (emotionally and cognitively) and accepting what he can't change. His prayers for guidance and self acceptance have helped dramatically. His spiritual growth has led him to a new and challenging job and a new assertive yet thankful way of living his life.

CHAPTER TWO

WE CAN'T PRAY AGAINST OUR BELIEFS

Cognitive psychotherapists tell us that we create our reality through our belief system. That is, through our experiences we come to believe certain things about life. These beliefs determine how we view further experiences and in fact help us create such experiences. This accounts for what Sigmund Freud called "the repetition compulsion." The earlier the beliefs are formed, the more repetitive these beliefs become, the more deeply they are held. For example, psychiatrists Guidano and Liotti, in their book *Cognitive Processes and Emotional Disorders*, explain the deeply held beliefs behind the major psychological problems. Fear is a major factor in most psychological problems.

Fearful people may have general anxiety or suffer from panic attacks. They believe that the world is a very dangerous place where no one will help them. They see themselves as very weak, vulnerable and utterly incapable in an emergency-and to people with panic attacks, life is a constant emergency. This idea coupled with the belief that nobody will help them, causes normal anxiety to spiral into sudden panic attacks. Their unconscious beliefs cause such attacks by generating images of being trapped somewhere out in the world, panicking, and not able to get home or to find safety. These images create panic, because the mind generates the same emotions if you imagine danger as if you are really in danger. If the panic is intense enough, we may irrationally avoid getting too far from home, lest a panic attack occur.

Such intense fear is very difficult to treat due to the severity of the symptom and the power of avoidance in calming the panic. The usual response of a person so dominated by fear is to run back home and stay there. Once home, the panic usually subsides. The fearful person learns to avoid more and more situations to remain calm. Gradually, he shrinks his world until he hates to leave home. If he does leave home, he must be free to run home at any minute because the panic attacks seem to come-"out of the blue." The worst place to be is stuck in traffic where one can't escape.

Why can't a fearful person pray to God to be freed from the prison of panic attacks and phobic avoidance of nearly everything? If this prayer were answered directly it would be going against the laws of cause and effect. You can't believe you are living in a hostile universe where you are weak and no one will help you and feel calm.

In order to really feel calm, you have to change your deeply held belief in fear. Therapists know that this problem must be approached on both the behavioral and cognitive levels. Gradually the person must be taught to calm down and then expose himself to the feared situations. As he begins to see he can be calmer in these situations, he is open to changing his deeply held, fearful beliefs. What is really needed is to change the deeply held, fearful belief that the ego has in being alone and helpless in the world. The fear dissolves when the deeply held belief changes.

Prayer can be helpful here, not as magic, but as an aid to changing the troublesome beliefs. One prayer I have found useful with people gripped by fear is, "Thank you God for helping me see that the world is safer than I thought." Or, simply, "The world is safer than I thought." As I said to one person, how many people *didn't get mugged last night.* Such prayers are much more effective if practiced in a meditative or self hypnotic state than from the usual conscious state of mind. It is very important to consider *why* the world is safer than they thought. It must make sense to both the conscious and unconscious mind of the afflicted person. For example, the world is safer because my medication is preventing the panic attacks. Or, it is safer because I have now learned how to calm myself down while sitting in traffic. It is at this point, the Higher Self or superconscious mind *can be reached through prayer* to provide the *strength* to make the actual change of deeply held belief. Now, the fearful person is no longer praying for a miracle against one's beliefs, but is praying for the strength to develop a new more functional belief. The ego or conscious mind never wants to let go of the old beliefs, no matter how outdated or dysfunctional they are. *Prayer, acting through the Higher Self, goes outside the ego system to make the change.* Still, the ego does not let up easily but aided by prayer, eventually relents and the belief is changed. Combined with "exposure" therapy, prayers will help the person to function better and more calmly. Of course, the true healing change is when we realize that the world is safe because all is really spirit. The danger is a creation of the fearful ego. The ego doesn't know what it is and fears its own destruction. Since the body holds the ego, it must be defended at all costs. Thus, when we stop identifying ourselves as bodies with egos and tune into spirit, we realize we are safe.

The Case of the Woman Who Lived in Fear

Debbie was trained from her earliest years to be fearful. Her mother was a fearful and overprotective person. Debbie became mother's little helper, spending a great deal of time helping mom, often staying in the house instead of going outside and playing. They spent several whole summers like this. Her mother improved with medication but Debbie had already learned her anxious lessons. She was very afraid of death and after several fainting spells, also became filled with fear of living fully. To Debbie, nothing was worse than getting caught in traffic and having a panic attack. She would go to great lengths to avoid experiencing out of control, panicky feelings. Eventually, the attacks became so bad that she had to take a leave from work.

During this leave time, I suggested she use the prayer, "the world is safer than I thought." She also learned self hypnosis and began to condition herself to calm down by using the cue words, *calm control.* Finally, she went on anti-depressant medication that also blocks panic attacks. The combination of spiritual, psychological, and biological therapy helped her greatly and she was able to return to work. Her task now is to convince her unconscious mind that it is now safe to be independent in the world. This requires a shift from ego thinking to Higher Self thinking. In other words, she must change her dysfunctional, symptom causing belief that the world is a dangerous place where nobody will help her, to a peace causing belief that all is well when she is allied with her Higher Self. She can make this shift via prayer, desensitization therapy, and medication. Once she changes the deeply held beliefs, she can go off the medication. The biggest mistake biological psychiatrists make is not working enough on the belief change and leaving patients on medication indefinitely. Many people can get off the medication if they work hard psychologically and spiritually.

Can You Pray Depression Away

Much work has been done with cognitive therapy for depression. Dr. Aaron Beck describes the typical "depressive triad", three beliefs that depressives commonly hold. These beliefs are: "Life is too difficult for me", "I am too weak to cope with life", and "there is no hope to feel any better in the future". If these beliefs are not changed, at some point, clinical (biological) depression will develop. This will be characterized by a despondent mood, lack of any pleasure in activities, feelings of guilt and worthlessness, difficulty sleeping, difficulty eating and extreme lethargy.

Again, we shall examine whether prayer can be of any help in the situation of clinical depression. The usual method would be to plead with an external, more powerful God to remove a condition which the person has "worked" long and hard to create-praying for God to go against his own laws to produce a "miracle" cure. Such a prayer would be for a powerful God to pump up the weak ego (low self-esteem) into a strong ego (high self-esteem). The reason this won't take place is that the real shift needed is from ego centered thinking to Spirit centered thinking. Bolstering self esteem is not the answer. A spirit centered person does not sit around ruing bad decisions and stewing in anger, fear and self hate. Thus, the depression is best healed by prayers that move one into a spirit centered consciousness.

The question is, how to help a depressed person move toward such Spirit centered thinking? A gradual approach is often best. The entry point is the cognitive aspect. You may begin the belief change with any part of the cognitive triad. For example, you may affirm, "I am stronger than I think," or "Thank you God for helping me see, I'm stronger than I think." Another entry point is, "I can cope better than I thought," or "Thank you God for helping me cope better than I thought." These last are examples of prayers, working toward the intermediate ideas, "I am strong", and "I cope well with the world." As you can see, dysfunctional beliefs are being replaced by *believable*, more functional beliefs. As the person gets stronger, hope develops. Then the real healing-the shift to a spiritual perspective can take place. Depression then lifts naturally. As we will see in later chapters, the spiritual reframe is the most radical reframe of all, choosing God as the focus and producing peace and eventually, *enlightenment*. An enlightened person is not depressed.

Prayer is not a one time experience, nor should it be something you do only when you are depressed or desperate. As we learn to pray daily, we have a rudder guiding us toward God's will. Eventually, when our life becomes a prayer, we realize that God's will and our will are identical. Initially, we may start a daily prayer process to solve our psychological problems. As our character gets stronger, we can learn *to take* full responsibility for our beliefs, actions and the results, our life. Then, and only then, can we *surrender to God's will.*

Actually, this is an *alliance* of the ego with the Higher Self. This is what the twelve step programs call "turning it over." The ego turns over responsibility for its depression or other problems to the Higher Self. We can only turn our problems and our lives over to God, (through the Higher Self), when we have accepted the responsibility for them. With this *healing alliance*, the ego accepts that it has actually caused the problems through its distortions and negative beliefs. As long as we cling to beliefs like, "it was just circumstances," or "it was his fault," etc., we cannot really turn it over. We can only turn over what is ours.

Belief Change Prevents Future Depression

In praying for belief change, we are accepting the responsibility for our lives. Instead of asking for pity from a Higher Being, we are working within the laws of the Higher Power. We are accepting that our beliefs are creating our problems through the law of cause and effect. We create depression through negative beliefs. We are harmonious with God when we pray for positive spiritual beliefs, from the Higher Self. By fully realizing our responsibility for our lives thus far, and then asking God for strength to correct our errors we are cooperating with spirit. This system works perfectly. Depressive and ego centered beliefs lead to pain and suffering. Positive and spirit centered beliefs lead to peace. Prayer is the bridge between the two.

CHAPTER THREE

PRAYER AFFIRMS THE TRUTH

In Biblical times, prayer was usually a plea to God for wishes and desires to be granted followed by a reason the wishes should be granted. Religious people had been assured that God was an all power-ful, external authority who would grant their wishes if they were worthy enough. If this were true, all good lawyers today would have their prayers answered because they built a good case. God would be more like the Chief Justice of the Supreme Court than a Deity.

This concept of God is reminiscent of what children are often taught. God is a super-being, sitting on a throne in a place called heaven, con-trolling everything. Yet, he is loving and wants to help if you would just ask. So we ask, and wonder why the wish is not granted. Perhaps we can accept that our prayer for wealth wasn't granted because that seems a bit selfish. But what about a simple prayer for healing? What kind of God would let me or my loved ones get sick or hurt. How could a lov-ing God let all the bad things of the world happen. How could earth-quakes, floods, disease and death be so rampant if God is so loving? Finally, if these things are just mistakes or oversights, why won't God correct the mistakes and make the world a better, safer place to live? When faced with so much pain, many people conclude that there isn't any God. Following this logic, in a way they are right. The truth is there isn't *that kind of God*.

God is not our humble servant, just waiting to do our bidding, such an idea violates natural law. *God is Something else.* When we experience what God truly is, we will not plead with God to have our desires granted, *we will affirm his/her greatness within us.* We will feel absolutely secure that we have nothing to worry about because God is *acting through us.* God is *individuating* in a multiplicity of ways through each of our lives. If each person really experienced and understood God, there would be little or no illness, disease or upheaval. In God's realm, if there was a physical world at all it would be more like the biblical Garden of Eden than the chaotic world we see. This garden is, of course, a metaphor for a world where all people would dwell in peace and harmony because they know they are merely individualization's of the great creative Spirit. The deepest truth is stated in the daily prayer of the Jews, "Hear O Israel, the Lord our God, the Lord is One." There it is. Admittedly few of us understand the implications of the prayer. It is a misunderstood, intellectual statement, not a felt Truth.

Affirmative Prayer Leads to Understanding the Truth

Pleading with a super-hero God actually leads us away from the truth, which is, that at the deepest level we are all one. That oneness can be called God, so in essence we are *all* part of God. At the spiritual level there is no separation, hence, we are God and don't know it.

The preceding short paragraph can easily be debated, pulled apart, or misunderstood. Let us resist the urge to do any of these things. Instead, let us inquire as to how we might proceed if it is true that we are all God. How do we leap from an intellectual concept to the enlightened experience of Cosmic Consciousness. Many mystics, like Joel Goldsmith, invite their students to understand the whole concept that we are God at once. I think that is rare to accomplish. Although it may be what the "born again" movement is about. What

I am proposing here is praying in an intentional, affirmative way as a gradual path to enlightenment.

A Gradual Path to Enlightenment

Buddhist writer Steven Levine entitled one of his books, *A Gradual Awakening*. He was referring to our ability to slowly become aware of our true selves. Not who we'd like to be but who we really are, right now. In all his books he encourages his readers to live fully in the moment, cherishing each minute of our lives. In this way, by accepting life, rather than trying to control it, we find God.

Pleading prayers are attempts to control things from our unique perspective. It assumes we know what we need, that our desires should be fulfilled, that we are in charge. It also assumes that we lack something, which could be graciously provided by a more powerful entity-a parental sort of God. It is as if we were saying, "Please give me my allowance so I can go to the movies." I may not have done my chores, but please give me the money anyway. The wise parent might suggest that the allowance will come when the chores are done. Eventually, the wise child stops pleading, does the chores, and affirms, "Thank you for my allowance." The allowance is, of course, right there and always has been. This may be a crude metaphor but there *are* Spiritual truths, and as we affirm them, they are manifested. As long as we beg for God to override his own laws, we are climbing up the wrong spiritual tree.

The Science of Mind and Affirmative Prayer

There are many philosophies which assert that *All* is really *One*. A good example is the *Science of Mind*, initiated by Ernest Holmes in the 1920s. Holmes asserted that the truth is that we are really one with God. The implications of that assertion are enormous. Prayers can be seen as affirmations of various aspects of the truth. For example, rather than pleading for money, we demonstrate abundance. We affirm, "My needs are being met, physically, emotionally and spiritually." As we persist in such an affirmation, things will begin to occur that will enable us to get all of our needs met. A new job may be offered, a new career may begin or someone we never thought of may offer assistance. Any form of abundance may appear, then we have to do our part to actualize it.

Holmes is quick to point out that the abundance part of his theology is not a "get-rich-quick" scheme. You don't just affirm wealth and it falls out of the sky. But if you affirm God's essential oneness, lovingness and justice, abundance will happen. You will get what you need. The essence of abundance is spiritual, not material. Sometimes it won't appear that you are getting what you need, but it *is* what you need. When you affirm the truth, the lessons will be taught, according to the blueprint set by your Higher Self. This is also termed God's Plan for you. Abundance is part of the plan, as soon as you realize what abundance is and what it is not.

No pleas are necessary for your plan to unfold, only an affirmation of truth and continued openness to the truth. Thus, if you affirm, "I live in an abundant universe." There are many possible outcomes. If you are already in tune with the belief that the universe will support you, a job may be offered. If your faith needs strengthening, someone may just give you the thing or money you need. But if you become greedy and already have what you need, the answer may be much more subtle. You may need to see that it already is an abundant universe and you just missed it. Perhaps you may happen to visit a poor country or neighborhood and thereby appreciate what you have. When properly understood, demonstrations tend to increase *faith*. And *faith dispels fear*. What is there to be afraid of after all? If God is merely trying to teach us about the nature of the universe, all we need to do is affirm the natural laws and go along with the program, watching in amazement as our needs for love, nurturance, sustenance and affiliation are filled. Sometimes the process can be slow, often leading us to erroneously give up on affirmative prayer.

The Problem Is Narcissism

As I discussed in my book *When Therapy Isn't Enough*, the blockage to our spiritual growth is *narcissism*, our immature selfishness. Due to the inevitable shortcomings of our primary care givers, and our innate predisposition's, we are to one degree or another impatient, egocentric, arrogant, and demanding. If our pleas or our affirmations do not lead to an immediate positive response, we often huff away angrily or sulk into despair. This is one reason so many people have trouble persisting in affirmative prayer. Thus, I encourage people to continue praying affirmatively and *daily* until their faith is bolstered by the inevitable demonstrated results. Eventually, the paradigm shift I alluded to earlier will begin to take place. Life becomes an exciting experiment. All the events of life, good and bad, are parts of *our Spiritual lesson plan*, leading to maturity, spiritual growth, and increases in faith, love, forgiveness and inner strength.

The Psychology of Affirmation

My introduction to the unconscious came through the study of psychology and hypnosis. I learned that you must never use a negative way of phrasing thoughts or ideas. The unconscious is very literal. If you program it negatively (as many parents do because of their own fear and guilt), it will produce negative results. If you tell your unconscious you want something to happen, it will create a state where you want it to happen. If you tell it something is happening now, it *is* happening now. The mind is very literal. Many people understand this partially and program their desires to happen soon. The trouble is, "soon" never comes. A much better approach is that it-whatever it may be is happening *now*. The mind then directs the body and all other interested "parties" that it indeed is happening now. Guess what, it tends to happen *now*. This is sometimes known as a "self fulfilling prophecy."

Philosopher Hans Vaihinger called this the philosophy of "as if." This philosophy, later adopted by The Beatles, suggests that we live "as if" we already have what we want. But what do you want? A problem free life? No one can consciously create a problem free life. That's not the way it's supposed to be. But, as we learn how to create our desired self-fulfilling prophecies according to spiritual law, we become more peaceful and harmonious. In other words, when what we want coincides with God's plan of spiritual growth we become more peaceful. We accept the "bad stuff" (illness, accident, death loss etc.) as part of the lesson and continue to affirm the spiritual laws. When we respond this way, our growth is quickened. This may not necessarily lead to a smooth or easy life but will lead to a spiritually fulfilling one. An example of this process is the Jewish prayer for the dead or kaddish. This prayer is actually an affirmation of God's greatness to bolster both the mourners and the departed spirit in the time of greatest need.

You may be wondering at this point how problems can lead us to the right type of affirmative prayers. The answer is that each problem contains the seeds of its spiritual solution. A case example will elucidate the point.

The Case of the Depressed Good Boy

Ned was the product of a fourteen year old mother and a forty-five year old father. As soon as he was born, his mother gave him over to his grandmother, "to keep her company." Neither mother nor grandmother gave little Ned much love or nurturance. Early on he learned to shut up, be good and not let his feelings or desires be known. By the time he was an adolescent he was depressed. His dark moods led to several clinical depressions and chronic feelings of unworthiness, low self esteem, inferiority and anxiety.

He was helped a little by psychotherapy, and anti-depressant medications but the chronic low mood, anxiety and passivity remained. By age 50, however, he had become involved with the A.R.E.(Association for Research and Enlightenment), a group based on the psycho-spiritual teachings of Edgar Cayce. This helped him too, but still he felt stuck, so he re-entered therapy and was encouraged to pray in an affirmative manner.

His favorite prayer was, "I'm powerful, I'm strong, I'm a man." This got him in touch with his natural assertiveness, his powerful Godly Higher Self. He also affirmed, "I'm just as good as anyone else." This led him to feel not superior but, OK. He eventually felt good enough to assert that he had just as much right as anyone to have a happy and good life.

Ned continues with these and other directed prayers, always phrased affirmatively-and often with thankfulness. He often adds, "Thank you God for helping me see that I'm powerful, strong, a man." He has been greatly helped by these prayers. He is now more assertive at work, in his relationships, and moving forward with his plans. His mood is more stable and lighter. He is also clear that he is on the road to recovery from his abusive childhood. He now sees all the earlier problems as opportunities that led him to where he is today.

Ned is affirming the strength to see that he is a worthy useful person. He isn't pleading for it, he is boldly stating that he *is* part of God, and as such he has strength and can see that he is OK just the way he is. This is a Universal Truth and affirming it connects him personally to God's strength. Each time he affirms it, it is better accepted by his personal unconscious, healing the narcissistic wounds of his childhood. Rather than just talking about it he is correcting his erroneous idea that he is worthless. As he connects to his Higher Self (God) he realizes that his mother and grandmother were mistaken. The Godly way is the healing way. He was taught that he was inferior and worthless. It became so much a part of him that he couldn't budge the negativity. However, by turning to the Higher Power, outside the ego system, he is gaining the strength to overcome his sense of inferiority, depression and passivity.

Countering Objections to Affirmative Prayer

The first objection to affirmative prayer often is that it doesn't seem like prayer. "Shouldn't you be asking politely for something in prayer? Shouldn't you have reverence, fear and awe of God?" There are many places in the Old Testament where we are told to fear God. We have learned that the word fear is better translated, "awe." Actually, by affirming rather than pleading, you do develop awe. It just isn't a fear filled awe. It's more like, "I can't believe how great God is." It is more of an affirming expression of awe. Pleading indicates a sense of inferiority that isn't true. If we are a part of the oneness of God we only need to affirm that and feel the positive sense of awe that goes with it.

The second objection to affirmative prayer is that it is arrogant. "How can you act like *you* are God? God is omnipotent and much more than any one person. This attitude is confusing the ego with the Higher Self. The ego would like to control everything but can't. It has no love, only fear. The Higher Self has no need to control anything. It understands the true nature of being and just lets the melodrama of life unfold the way it's supposed to. There is great humility in these affirmations. We become secure in the knowledge that at the deepest level, we *are* all one. It has no fear, only love.

Replacing Pleas with Gratitude

Some people are so used to begging and pleading with God that they have a hard time phrasing prayers any other way. I teach them that any plea can be replaced with a statement of gratitude. "Please heal my illness" can be replaced with "Thank you for healing my illness." This small point is vitally important. The gratitude assumes that the prayer *is already answered.* It is important to point out however, that the gratitude must be heartfelt and that the prayer is still processed according to psychological and spiritual law.

We spend the vast majority of our lives in touch with the psychological level which interacts with the physical level through the law of cause and effect. Thoughts and emotions affect the body through the endocrine system. Thus, you may not necessarily cure your cancer by just saying, "thank you for healing my cancer." This is what transpersonal theorist Ken Wilber meant when he called such affirmations, "jumping a level." He was very frustrated because his wife, Treya had been criticized by her New Age friends for giving herself cancer. Her friends did not understand that cancer is a complex disease and that just as she didn't give herself cancer, she could not just cure it physically by prayer.

In Wilber's moving tribute to his wife, it is clear that she was healed emotionally and spiritually, even though she died of the cancer. The physical and psychological are connected but not identical. Psychology will not heal cancer directly, but, by repeating an affirmation you will be led where you have to go for the healing to take place. It might be a surgeon, a naturopath, a healer or a slow process mediated by your immune system. Most importantly, the healing, either emotional or physical can take place through interaction with the metaphysical levels of consciousness. Healing of some sort *will* take place when heartfelt prayers of gratitude are affirmed. Attitudes can always change. Psychiatrist Victor Frankl, a concentration camp survivor called this attitudinal healing. In the rare cases where we are completely aligned with the Spiritual level, miraculous physical healings can take place. It is important to realize though that the absence of a spectacular physical healing does *not* mean the prayers weren't answered. The prayers were processed at the psychological and/or metaphysical level producing a different type of healing, and emotional and Spiritual healing. *All of our prayers are answered.* We just need to learn how to recognize different types of answers.

The Case of the Timid Artist

Sergio was a fifty-two-year-old artist with an obvious problem: two large tumors growing on his face. One was on his ear, one on his lip. His physician wanted to remove them but he had a phobia of anesthesia and would not permit it. This was a potentially life threatening situation as well as a serious impairment to his appearance. Yet, he could not overcome his fear. The tumors grew steadily bigger. In desperation, he came in asking for hypnosis to overcome his phobia. We had several sessions to discuss our approach before hypnosis was initiated. Sergio was a spiritual man and open to prayer as well as hypnosis. Thus, we decided to combine the two. In the deeply relaxed state of hypnosis, I gave him post-hypnotic suggestion to repeat affirmative prayers until the problem was resolved. The prayer was, "Thank you God for removing the tumors in the best way possible." There were other suggestions that the tumors might shrink and disappear or that he might just go to a surgeon and have them removed. He continued to pray despite no shrinkage of tumors and no inclination to face his fears and go to a surgeon.

At this point, he went on vacation to his native country, Brazil. One day, while passing a street sign for a surgeon, he impulsively walked in and allowed the Brazilian surgeon to remove the tumors. He had no idea why he suddenly had courage, he just did it. The key point is that his prayers did not specify how the tumors were to be removed. He had humbly thanked God and turned the problem over to a Higher Power. When it was time to act, he just did it.

Directive vs. Non-Directive Prayer

A group called the Spindthrift foundation engages in prayer research. In numerous experiments with plants growing under various conditions, prayer was shown to aid the plant's growth. For those of us who believe in prayer this isn't surprising. The somewhat surprising result was that non-directive prayer was significantly more helpful that directive prayer. In the Spindthrift plant experiments, plants were stressed by giving them salt water. Both types of prayer helped the plants, but the prayers for the greater good of the plants were most effective. This greater effectiveness of non-directive prayer has important applications for people. Apparently, it is better to assert the best outcome for all concerned than to specify that a certain result be obtained. It was better in the case above to pray for tumor removal than for a specific method of removal. It might have been even better to pray for the best outcome for the patient and all people concerned. Of course, this takes great faith that God, the Higher Power or even our own unconscious knows better what is needed to result than we do. The ego cannot see the greater context; It wants what seems to be best for itself. No matter how obvious the desire is, only the Higher Power has the wider context. Thus, the most effective prayers are affirmative, non-directive, grateful and heartfelt.

It may be hard to be non-directive, particularly in the case of illness but the most effective prayers are the ones phrased that way. A good compromise in healing prayers is, "Thank you God for healing—(my) body, mind and spirit, in the best way possible, for all concerned." This still gives us the comfort of asking for a bodily healing while taking into account that every illness is also a communication which has psychological and spiritual components. The Higher Power sees the wider picture. The patient and loved ones frequently cannot. Sometimes, an emotional healing also produces a physical healing. Other times, as in the case of Treya Wilber (Ken Wilber's wife) the healing might be death. This may make no sense to the western mind. But the Buddhist concept implies that there is a continued existence of the soul and that when bodily death is meant to happen, it happens. On Earth, we all die at some point. Again, we must realize that there is a Higher Power that knows and sees more than we do. Our prayers shouldn't order God what to do, they should affirm a greater level of knowledge, power and love than we currently possess.

Does God Give Some People Cancer?

I had the following conversation with a friend last night. He asked me, "Do you believe God gives some people cancer?" "No", I replied, automatically (surprised at the ease of my own answer). "Well then, can God heal cancer?" "Yes" I replied, with equal speed. "Then you're saying he can cure it but doesn't cause it? Yes. "Why do I think that way?

There are as many opinions about what causes cancer as there are people. It just isn't so simple that it can be refined to one cause. What we do know is that cancer is a runaway growth of cells that if not checked will eventually kill the body. This inspires fear in most people, fear of a loss of a loved one, fear of a loss of one's self. Fear is on a level where psychology and spirituality meet. Though there is no guarantee that the physical cancer can be cured, the fear behind it can be healed. Fear can be cured by faith. *Absolute faith casteth out fear.* The part of us that is afraid is the ego, that socially created aspect of ourselves that doesn't know what it is, but wants to survive at any cost.

Transpersonal philosopher Michael Washburn tells us that the ego is insecure, extraverted and afraid by nature-a temporary focus of awareness that has overstepped its usefulness. Out of fear of its own obliteration by the death of the body, the ego gives rise to worry, fear and anxiety which than helps destroy the very body it is trying to save. Prolonged stress can lead to over activation of the immune system which can be a factor in creating the runaway cell growth that is cancer. In combination with other factors, the fearful, insecure ego has a lot more to do with causing cancer than God. God is that silent presence far beneath (above?) the ego that wants nothing more than for the ego to recognize oneness and ally with it.

Washburn tells us that at a certain point in life we must surrender to "the Ground of Being" and re-integrate our personality in a higher way. He calls this, "regression in the service of transcendence." The ground of being (God) is, in essence a loving nurturing source of all being, not a controlling, punishing dictator. Thus, God does not give us cancer or any other illness, rather this illness is one possible outcome of our difficulty with re-integrating ourselves on a spiritual level.

I can hear the objections to this concept as I write. Are you saying that spiritual people should not get sick? No! Otherwise, pious people would live indefinitely and harsh materialists would all die young. Each immortal soul has a different agenda in life. We must all begin to understand where we are. The trouble is not with God. The loving energy source wants nothing more than peace, love and harmony because it *is* nothing more than peace, love and harmony. However, in our ignorance most of us are very ego and body based, this is the human condition. In other words, due to the realities of human upbringing we all have over-inflated and or terrified egos. This is our narcissism. The problem, for almost all of us, is narcissism.

Through prayer and meditation we can deal more effectively with our damaged egos. For some people, serious illness is part of the learning process. This is *not* a conscious decision. Thus, we do *not* give ourselves cancer. Nor does *God* give us cancer. Cancer is one possible part of the learning process called life. We are learning to become more loving, compassionate beings. In order to do this we must go through some sort of pain. Pain is necessary, suffering is optional. Jane Roberts tells us that the "only purpose of suffering is to learn how to stop suffering." She says we can stop suffering when we realize the nature of reality. Washburn tells us that we must face our early hurts, take responsibility for our attitudes and "surrender to the ground of being." What does this mean?

What Are We Surrendering

We are surrendering fear, pride and self will, in that order. I believe that all human beings have to go through this process. It is the way life is supposed to be. The fear, which Dr. Karen Horney called, "basic anxiety" is formed as we go through the developmental process of growing up. Horney thought this occurred only with neurotic individuals. She felt that basic anxiety was a result of narcissistic, self-absorbed parents who were unable to make the child feel really loved. Her only mistake was in not realizing the prevalence of narcissism. In one sense, the problem is narcissism, in our parents and in ourselves. We cannot remake our parents, but we can heal ourselves of the wounds they unwittingly (in most cases) inflicted upon us. This is the process of spiritual growth.

Washburn tells us that it is normal to develop fear during childhood. Part of this is the fear of the terrors of the outer world. The rest is fear of the world of the unconscious, especially the "lower unconscious." The so called lower part of the unconscious *is* filled with fierce repressed emotions: anger, guilt, jealousy etc. We have repressed these feelings to please our parents and peers, to become socialized beings, acceptable to society. By the time we are teens, we have repressed most of our unconscious, especially the unacceptable feelings. These repressed feelings become our "shadow." We project the shadow on others, blaming them for these bad feelings. Washburn calls this "original repression." He might just as well have called it "original sin."

Unfortunately, we "throw away the baby with the bath water." We repress the spiritual part of the unconscious (Higher Self) along with the painful lower unconscious. We convince ourselves that we are nothing but separate, material beings, doomed to die and be extinguished. In short, we lose our connection to the God within us and put all our energy into material success. Thus, we live in fear of failure, loss and death.

The answer lies in reconnecting to our Higher Spiritual Selves, or in other words, surrendering to God. A more palatable way of putting this is to create an alliance with the Higher Self. Unfortunately, the path to the "Higher Self" goes through the forbidden territory of the lower unconscious filled with hurt, anger, fear, guilt, hate and inferiority. It is usually easier (we think) to ignore the forbidden unconscious and our Higher Self and just believe that we are separate finite material beings-bodies, directed by our egos.

Interestingly, the most successful people (externally) are the most convinced that there is nothing else in the Universe. They have pushed the unseen spiritual world so far away that they have totally forgotten their source. Material success has bolstered the illusion that there is nothing else but the "real" material world.

It is normal to go though early adulthood focused on external success. However, as Jung mentioned, after the age of thirty-five or forty we begin to sense that there is something missing. That missing link is God, hidden in the unconscious. The psychologically more damaged people have more to fear than the overtly successful (but often more repressed) people. Fear of the powerful repressed emotions sometimes keeps them from the spiritual search. The less damaged people are more successful in the world. Paradoxically, their problem is that they are not in enough pain to go spiritually searching. However, many people from both groups *do* embark on the spiritual search-even though the path goes right through the pain in the lower unconscious. Sometimes, a dark period occurs spontaneously. Other times when we initiate prayer or meditation we enter a difficult period called the "dark night of the soul."

The Dark Night of the Soul

Carl Jung himself went through a dark night of the soul that lasted from 1913-1919. Jung was deeply disturbed and overwhelmed by his unconscious during these years. However, by sticking to a strict regimen of self analysis, while maintaining his ties to reality (home, family, clientele), he was able to utilize this period as one of tremendous spiritual growth. During this time he began to "channel" various spiritual guides through "automatic writing." One of his guides, named Philemon, unconsciously moved Jung's hand in Fourteenth Century script, until he had written 1,330 pages of what was later called, "the Red Book." This material formed the backdrop to all Jung's later writing. He spent the rest of his life scientifically validating what he had written during these years. Thus, Jung was able to blend intuitive knowledge with scientific validation. He became known as the Wise Old Man from Kusnacht. Shortly before his death in 1961, he was asked by the BBC if he believed in God. His answer should be a goal for all of us. He said, "I don't believe, *I know*!"

Affirming Your Spiritual Alliance

What does affirmation have to do with surrender and spiritual alliance? There is a two-step process of affirmation that ultimately will lead to surrender to the Ground of Being (God). First, we must recognize that we are creating our reality according to our beliefs. We must affirm that it is not an external God, bad luck, bad karma, bad genetics or bad circumstances that is making us unhappy. We are unhappy because we are stubbornly insistent on solving our problems ourselves without seeing how our negative beliefs and attitudes are ruining us. As the comic book character Pogo once said, "We have seen the enemy and it is us." Our ego and character are formed through experience. As young children, we tend to deny the law of cause and effect. Whatever happens is not our doing: "I didn't do it, she did it," and so on.

As we mature, we take more and more responsibility for our lives. Yet, there are always portions of our reality that we insist on projecting onto other people, chance, or God. Thus, if I get sick, it's because there is a "bug going around." It wouldn't be that I am run down from too much activity and need some enforced silence and rest! If I lose money, it's because "the market or business is bad." It's not because I made some bad decisions, do research, or didn't network enough. If I have a fight with my wife, it's her fault; I didn't do anything to provoke her. I could go on and on but the point is, *the more responsibility you take for your life, the better off you are.* You are then in the fortunate position of being *able* to surrender to or join with the Higher Power. How can you surrender what you don't own? Own it first, turning the problem over from the ego to the Higher Self. Many spiritual systems stress the importance of surrender, but I cannot emphasize enough how important it is to own your responsibility *before* you surrender. This is what transforms surrender into a spiritual alliance.

The most enraging line in Jane Roberts' book is, "You create your own reality through your conscious and unconscious beliefs and feelings...period, there is no other rule." Skeptics immediately start coming up with scenarios that *prove* that this isn't true. These exceptions generally include helpless children and victims of "natural disasters." Now, I certainly sympathize with the plight of children with hurtful parents, and think concerned adults should do everything to help them on a societal as well as individual basis. Most of these children become damaged adults. At that point it becomes our duty to help them use the trauma as entry points to the spiritual growth process. Therapists have traditionally tried to help people get in touch with their anger etc. Often, however, the next step, forgiveness, is never reached. Those of us who are healers must help in both the psychological *and* spiritual dimensions of recovery. This includes helping people see that even if they were once victims of abuse, they can take themselves through the hurts into healing Spirituality. This includes taking *responsibility for the continued nursing of grievances.* We must encourage people to go through anger and hate to the healing power of love and forgiveness. This is true even if the abusers remain clueless and never heal themselves. This is true even if the perpetrators are long dead.

Now, the point of entry remains getting in touch with the hurt, anger, rage depression etc. and work *through it* to the point where forgiveness and love are possible. Denial of the feelings will not work. This requires going beyond your own version of the dark night of the soul on the path to spiritual growth. Take responsibility for your portion of the situation, then join with the Higher Self in surrender and forgiveness.

What are we surrendering? Only, our negative thoughts feelings and behaviors. What are we affirming? Only the power of God to heal the negativity with love. In terms of *A Course In Miracles*, we are going outside the ego system to heal ourselves. A simple affirmative prayer will do:

Thank You God for giving me the strength to release my anger, hate and guilt and leading me to love and forgiveness. I hereby surrender my negative thoughts, feelings and behaviors. Thank you for replacing them according the highest Spiritual principles.

CHAPTER FOUR

PRAY FOR CHARACTER CHANGE

Most People are used to praying for the *things* they *think* they need. Health, more money and romantic love head the list of things people want. What people don't realize is that these things will appear if they are really needed, and we will help ourselves by following spiritual law. Otherwise we are actually asking God to violate his own spiritual laws to get us out of jams we have created ourselves—consciously or unconsciously.

The key concept here is the general lack of awareness of how much of our lives we do create ourselves. A few examples will elucidate this point. The aforementioned situation of Hank is a case in point. You'll recall Hank wanted to kill himself because he couldn't get into a rewarding intimate relationship. In the beginning of therapy he wasn't oriented toward prayer at all. But even if he had been, it would not have been productive to pray directly for a partner. The problem was inside, not outside himself. Eventually, Hank realized that he was actively avoiding relationships because of his guilt, shame and fear about his sexuality. He felt unworthy of being loved because he had been trained to think little of himself. He felt even more unworthy of sexual love because his sexual impulses were connected only with brief shameful encounters. His prayers needed to be directed not to finding a partner but to healing the shame. Thus, I encouraged him to redirect his efforts toward healing his shame first. ("Thank You God for helping me see that I am *worthy* of a loving close relationship.") As his shame was healed he naturally moved into a loving close relationship. One could also thank God by asking for removal of shame but it is best to approach the healing by naming what we have to move *toward*, rather than what we have to move away from.

Part of Hank's healing of shame was his development of a Buddhist orientation: seeking enlightenment. He began to look at his desires as preferences rather than absolute needs. "All results are O.K. "became his motto. He became more and more willing to do the things he needed to do to meet appropriate lovers. He no longer prayed for a miracle induced by God. He prayed to *look at things differently*. This is essentially the prayer for guidance urged by *A Course in Miracles*. His life became the miracle. He prayed for character development as the solution of his problems. He did not focus on a particular result. Hank became convinced that any result was O.K. as long as he continued to grow Spiritually. Amazing things happened in all areas of his life. With little effort, he found a much better, more creative job. As problems surfaced he transcended his initial fears quickly and shifted into the spiritual mode. His questions to his Higher Self became: what can I learn from this situation? What is my part in using this seemingly troublesome situation in a positive way? Hank has truly switched his orientation to life, from shame based materialism to love based spirituality. His prayers are for character change and a different point of view, not things.

A Brief Theoretical Excursion

What can we learn from Hank that can help us? Hank is a classic example of what psychotherapist Alice Miller called "the drama of the gifted child." He was severely psychically wounded continually as a child, leading to a shame based existence. He became a dedicated materialist, using his scientific education against himself. He looked for success and achievement to feel good. He was so bright he used many of my early therapeutic attempts to help him against himself. At times I would try to create therapeutic "double binds." These are carefully worded questions, designed so that no matter which way one answers, the result is therapeutic. For example, I would say something like would you like to feel better now or later...I was trying to help him improve his depressed mood. He would say, "I see by your wording you are trying to trick me..." He so hated himself, he resisted his own therapy and denied the existence of a God.

According to transpersonal theorist Ken Wilber, Hank suffered severe "developmental lesions" early in life. The result was a weakened set of "psychic structures." These structures are likened by Wilber to the rungs on a ladder. The conscious self is (so to speak) climbing the ladder of psychological and spiritual growth. If the rungs are weakened by anger, guilt and shame, "lesions" occur. A fall from the "ladder" (psychic structures) could result in depression or even suicide. Where does prayer fit into this structure?

I believe that prayer can strengthen the psychic structures that were damaged in childhood, enabling the depressed person to first express, then let go of the anger, guilt and shame that fuels depression. This then frees the "ego" (climber of the ladder) to ally with the Higher Self and become more loving, giving, forgiving and mature. It is important not to confuse the psychic structures (ladder) with the ego (climber). Strong structures are necessary to live in the world, enabling the ego to then surrender and join with the Higher Self, choosing peace. We all start life as part of God, thus we are naturally good. But this goodness is inevitably impaired by the hurts of growing up—slowing, sometimes stopping the psycho-spiritual maturing process. Sin (an archaic archery term for missing the mark) and evil are only errors in judgment caused by the developmental lesions of growing up. It is as if we are saying, "I will not mature any more until I go back to childhood and am treated better." This immaturity is an ego developmental problem. It leads to the "sin" of the immediate gratifications that seem like answers: addictions, overindulgence in sensory pleasure etc. This immaturity cannot be solved by the neurotic ego itself which is too involved in either forgetting its spiritual source or nurturing the hurt. Immaturity can only be solved by using the resulting problems as triggers for Spiritual growth. This is where prayer comes in.

Hank prayed for himself to heal the hurts of the past. He also worked at expressing his anger at his father, on the road to eventual forgiveness. He went beyond the hurt, shamed ego and asked for the strength to move toward enlightenment. As the shame dissipated, he became strong enough so that he *could* pursue relationships without fearing rejection or failure. For the Spiritually mature person, following the guidance of the Higher Self (or God, or the Holy spirit) there is no such thing as rejection or failure. There is only learning and moving to a higher level of psychological and spiritual development. Even temporary setbacks are utilized in the service of transcendence. Nor is there really rejection, since the puffed up, oversensitive ego is no longer in control. The person who has been strengthened by prayer has allied with the Higher Self. Washburn would say we have "surrendered to the Ground of Being."

When God or the Ground of Being is in charge, there is no rejection. From the point of view of the Higher Self, we couldn't care less what another person, operating out of a judgmental ego thinks. A person being led by his ego will always be insecure. It is your choice which path to follow. Your prayers can be directed to gain the strength to wisely choose the Godly path.

Prayer can help enormously to strengthen us enough so that we can make different choices. It is no accident that spiritually based therapies (e.g. 12 step programs) help addicts. Addiction is such a powerful lure that only the Higher Power can lead us away from the ego's demand for addictive substances. The insecure, neurotic ego just wants its stuff. It never heals anything. But, once we have gained some strength, we can choose to ally the ego with the Higher Self. This is the surrender to God that Michael Washburn talks about. It is the "turning our lives over to God" that our Western Religions talk about. When we turn to the Higher Power, we become strong enough to resist quick fixes. It takes a mature person to wait and develop the much greater happiness of unification with God through prayer and meditation. To the immature person, the quick fix seems infinitely preferable to a possible greater happiness later. Prayer can help us move past the early hurts that lead us to make unhealthy selfish choices. It can help us move toward surrender, love, peace and harmony.

The Gradual Path to Enlightenment

Prayer for character change is a gradual path to enlightenment. Prayer provides the strength to change, sometimes even when the flesh is weak and the ego is tricky. Prayer can provide the strength to break through resistances in psychotherapy. I have often noted that patients who pray regularly for themselves have much less resistance to change than patients who do not. Psychiatrist Charles Whitfield noted that patients who had a daily spiritual practice continued to abstain from drugs and alcohol much longer and had a much better life adjustment than patients who had only psychotherapy.

Back to Wilber

Wilber's basic model of the psyche begins with the same psychic stages posited by traditional developmental psychology. Thus, he notes that the earlier the psychic wound, the more serious the psychological disturbance. He also notes that different types of therapy are more appropriate for people who are wounded at different times of life. For example, an unstable borderline personality needs support, encouragement and compassion to help heal the impaired lower basic structures. In other words, a person with a "weak ego" is unstable and flounders emotionally. They also are terrified and their defenses against the terror aren't working. Without supportive, encouraging assistance such a person's emotions are too overwhelming to make a strong alliance with Spirit and thereby mature. On the other hand, "neurotics" (those wounded at later ages) have repressed their feelings *too much*. Washburn would say their original repression has worked too well. They are just as afraid as people with weak egos but they are much less aware of the fear. Thus, they need therapy that helps them re-learn how *to feel* and open up to their own needs and desires. Then they need to re-open to the unconscious Ground of Being where God connects to us.

Different kinds of prayer are appropriate at different times of life. Thankful, petitionary prayer directed toward strength and ability to tolerate and lessen symptoms may be the most appropriate mode for people overwhelmed by emotion. Though this can be useful at any level, it can be of vital assistance during panic attacks or agitated depression. The importance of alliance with the Higher Self cannot be stressed enough. An overwhelmed person can be greatly helped by turning the management of extreme symptoms over to the Higher Power. This can eliminate what Dr. Claire Weekes calls "second fear"—fearing the physical sensations of fear—until "first fear" can be healed by the Higher Power.

For people at "higher" levels of development (wounded later, thus neurotic), it may be more appropriate to spend more time with prayers of adoration and contemplation (meditation). This practice aids in surrendering the defense system which has been overdeveloped out of fear of the forbidden unconscious thoughts and feelings. Though most people benefit from meditation, there is a strong research literature indicating that some people get *symptomatically* worse from meditating. They may not be strong enough yet in their lower structures to tolerate the energy rush (sometimes called the rising of the *kundalini*) that sometimes occurs with meditation. Prayers to develop faith and overcome fear are also helpful for the over controlled neurotic. These prayers may be used as a prelude to meditation.

Growing Spiritually

Prayer for character change can do no harm and may be very helpful in the overall road to enlightenment. Simple prayers for *things* frequently fail because they slow down or even stop Spiritual growth. God knows this, but people frequently can't see this in the immediacy of their needs. They often are confused about what God's Plan is for them. Though the specifics may vary greatly, in general, there is only one answer. *God wants you to grow spiritually.* He-She wants you to be more loving, kind, compassionate and understanding. He-She doesn't want a phony sweetness though. God wants you to develop the insight and the wisdom to *really* feel love and compassion for all sentient beings. He-She wants you to experience your (Jungian) shadow and integrate it. He-She wants you to be happy, joyful, spontaneous and genuine. And God wants you to do this *while you are alive.* Heaven is a resting place. Earth is where we do our Spiritual work. We can experience heaven while on Earth. But it requires work, courage and true insight. Don't waste your time here. Use it well for Spiritual growth. Use your pain and problems as springboards for the growth. Whatever problems life gives you, use them to develop your Spiritual capacity. The eventual goal is enlightenment. When enlightened, you are no longer really concerned with your self. You will be happy to reunify with God in the best way possible.

This is why Wilber's final step in spiritual growth is unification. He sees the self as a "transitional structure." At the lower levels, you need it (the self) desperately. The more you gain Spiritual insight however, the less you need this insecure deluded ego self. The key for everyone is to take the vital step of turning to the Higher Power by starting to pray in whatever way is most comfortable for you. Don't focus on results, they will flow naturally. There is usually a time lag in the results of prayer and character change. Pray for patience to allow the time to pass. I teach beginning meditators to say before starting, "Here goes nothing." Then do your prayers.

A Course in Miracles

A Course in Miracles is a wonderful series of three books designed to correct the misperceptions of Christ's teachings. My first Course teacher, Diane Gusic, taught us that "the ego is the enemy." This was a very hard teaching to swallow for a trained psychologist. After much soul searching, I believe I understand what she meant now. The ego is largely a product of emotionally charged interactions with others. It is necessary to function in this world, *but* it almost inevitably becomes deluded due to the weaknesses caused by the perceived hurts of its development. If it is too weak, it feels unprotected from the strong emotions in the unconscious. People with such weak egos may be aware of the Spiritual level, but they are too overwhelmed to make an alliance with the Higher Self. People with so called "strong egos" have the opposite problem. They are also afraid but they have forgotten about or denied their Spiritual source to keep the fear completely out of awareness. They have paid a high price to shut out their fear: They have shut out God. Whether you have a weak ego or a strong ego, low self esteem or high self esteem, the ego stands in the way of our true happiness. It is small wonder that many of us remain insecure and feel unloved. We rarely think of forming a Spiritual alliance with God. If we do, the ego looks for ways to derail our spiritual search.

Dr. Karen Horney would say that our level of confusion is between real self and idealized image. A neurotic ego seeks to glorify a grandiose, idealized version of itself. In identifying this idealized image as our real self, we make a fundamental error. Our real self is identical with Spirit. Most of us are haunted by fear and very reluctant to ally ourselves totally with spirit. We are fearful primarily because we have forgotten our Spiritual source. We forgot our Spiritual source because it was buried beneath repressed human emotions, to try to please our parents. We eventually streamline our idealized image, designed to please our parents into what is usually called our ego. This ego is bound to be insecure, even if we had great parents and an ideal upbringing. We would have to face the ultimate fear, annihilation or death of this curious creation, our ego. We identify this ego with our body and will go to great lengths to preserve it. We think we are nothing but an ego in a body and that when our body dies, we die. This is the great error the Course is trying to correct. When we forget who we really are we are fearful and insecure. When we move toward our Real Self, Spirit, we are peaceful and happy. By virtue of being human, we still develop a separate ego which we need in this world *but* it is *imperative that we do join with the Higher Self and form a spiritual alliance* in order to eradicate the illusory fear of death that haunts so many of us. The only way to really face fear of death is spiritually. It is only with a spiritual alliance that we realize that it was only the ego part of us that was afraid. The Higher Self is always eternal and always knew it.

Horney's feeling was that "neurosis" was caused by basic anxiety or fear that our self centered parents would ignore our needs and let us die. Though Horney doesn't mention it, the fear really stems from the young child's rudimentary identification with the body and ego. The less nurturing the parents are, the more cut off the young child is from Spirit. It becomes solely concerned with physical and ego survival. In her book, *Neurosis and Human Growth*, Dr. Horney gives a brilliant exposition of the dynamics of the neurotic ego. Just as *A Course in*

Miracles states about the ego, Horney's neurotic ego will always lead us in the wrong direction. Horney's neurotic ego tells us to attack anyone who threatens to reveal that we are not ideal or perfect. The neurotic ego wants us to think we are great and innocent. Others are seen as impediments to our happiness, and righteousness. It matters not what our version of perfect is. The neurotic ego promises that we are either there or almost there. This leads to tremendous tension, strain and misery trying to be our version of ideal. Horney urges us to accept ourselves as we actually are and actualize our *Real Self.* The Real Self is what we become when we ally with the Higher Self or Holy Spirit that the Course encourages us to turn to for guidance.

The Pathwork Material

The Pathwork material is another wonderful teaching. It is very similar to Dr. Horney's teaching. The writer was Eva Pierrakos, who revealed her teachings, in German in 1958. One look at Pierrakos' teachings gives us the idea that Horney may well have inspired Pierrakos to continue her teachings. The early lectures are a re-hash of Horney's theory: People defend their fragile egos by moving toward, away or against others. Later Pathwork teachings, however, are more spiritually oriented than Horney's works.

My favorite lesson from the Pathwork is the one on prayer. We are urged to pray at least one half hour per day to overcome our fear, pride and self will. Fear is seen as the root cause of all problems. Neurotic pride is the cover up for the fear. It is the ego's way of deluding us into thinking the ego's ways of fear and defense are correct. In other words, we are actually proud of our idealized image of ourselves. "Self will" is the end result of this fear and pride, resulting in selfish goals and behavior.

"Those who do not pray will never be able to act and fulfill themselves as can those people who have learned the power of proper prayer."*Pathwork lecture #36*

This *Pathwork* lecture urges us to persevere in analysis until we can see the whole picture of our unhealthy patterns. We are also told that prayer is an excellent means of learning to concentrate on essentials; love, forgiveness, faith, in a positive manner.

Prayer helps us see the chasm between our thoughts and feelings. By clarifying our problems and concentrating on the spiritual antidotes, we are told that we can heal our problems until our life becomes a prayer. The point of view of this book is that our life is *already a prayer*, it is just that our prayers are so chaotic, negative and unfocused, we can't see how we create all these problems we don't want. By learning to focus better, concentrate, and look at the Spiritual antidotes to our human problems, our lives will become more *meaningful*.

Pathwork urges us to remove fear, self will and pride. We are told to ask that these problems be replaced with faith, love and humility. We are urged to pray for the ability to accept whatever pain and fear arise as we go through our life process, moving toward spiritual goals and values. We are advised not to expect ourselves to be perfectly good. Rather, we should keep praying, do the best we can and accept the results. We need to accept that pain and fear are our *teachers*. We are urged to ask in prayer which is more real: the idealized image or the real self?, the lower self or the Higher Self? The answers will come but not usually in a dramatic way. We need to learn how to see answers in small life events. Thus, we are urged to turn to God in prayer for guidance, even with small problems and uncertainties. The result will be Spiritual growth *and* a change in what we desire. In the end, we will be more alive and less ego centered.

We are urged by *The Pathwork* material to realize the power of our thoughts and feelings. Thoughts can be controlled more directly than feelings. Thus, we are encouraged to accept our feelings, which will lead us to the underlying negative beliefs which can be changed gradually. Positive thinking is a later step in character change. First, we must accept the pain that results from our negative thinking according to the law of cause and effect. Then, we can change our beliefs and think more positively. This system of gradually changing negative beliefs is similar to the "working through" phase of psychoanalysis and the belief change of cognitive therapy. However, *The Pathwork* goes beyond these traditional modes of therapy and becomes similar to the Seth material of Jane Roberts in that eventually we realize that we are much *more* than we think we are. In other words when we are to realize we are Spiritual Beings, temporarily in a body, we can move ourselves into realms where we don't need pain for our development.

As we can see by the forgoing discussion, prayer for character change is a vital element in the process of Spiritual growth. Rather than looking for magical answers from a superior being, we turn to the *God in each of us*, for the strength to become responsible enough to make the necessary changes in ourselves, heal our narcissistic wounds and grow Spiritually toward a life of greater love, peace and harmony. In order to do this, we must strengthen our faith. It is this aspect of character change that we turn to now.

Chapter Five

Deepening Your Faith-How To Pray

As long as we think and feel that we are *nothing* but separate, physical creatures, we will at some level be plagued by fear and guilt. Few people trace these feelings to their choice to ignore their innate spirituality. They may be aware of feeling separated, abandoned or hated by *people*, without relating these fears to *God*—for, at the deepest level fear and guilt are about God. If we deny our connection to God, the universe feels random and dangerous. Belief in a vengeful God or that there is no God will create *fear of* the loss of our existence-death. These painful feelings can take many forms: loneliness, abandonment, separation from loved ones, creating a terror of complete obliteration and annihilation of ourselves. This terror is a result of the ego, which doesn't know what it is, convincing us that its demise will remove us completely. If we have lost touch with our Spiritual Self we may agree. This is what fear is all about.

Without God or a belief in a separate angry God, can cause feelings of guilt about a host of things: not being "good enough", not trying hard enough, that we are irresponsible or bad, and ultimately that we stand alone. This is what guilt *seems* to be about, but at the deepest level we feel guilty about separating from the source of our being, God. As Washburn says, in repressing the unconscious, we have thrown out the good with the bad. We have cut off our connection to the Ground of Being. Just as we need to feel connected with our family and community, we need to develop interdependence with a Higher Being in order to be peaceful and happy. The formerly chaotic world seems better once we are joined with God.

Very few families teach *interdependence*. I use this word to connote a healthy ability to function independently sometimes and to lean on others when necessary. Some families teach children never to leave the family emotionally, thus causing *guilt* when normal independence and development is desired. Other families teach exaggerated independence, the need to make it totally on one's own. Both are really metaphors for our relationship to God.

Exaggerated dependency leads to guilt, especially as one matures and wants to develop healthy independence. Guilt requires punishment and if we think we did anything wrong (like "leaving" the enmeshed family) we have a need to be punished, as we were by our parents. The motto of the neurotically enmeshed family is, "I'll hate you if you leave me"-keeping the children totally dependent and giving rise to anger and resentment. The anger is mixed *with guilt about the anger*. These emotions are connected with depression. Thus, it is important to become conscious of these toxic beliefs and feelings, so we can transcend them.

We hold these toxic family-based beliefs even deeper, at the Spiritual level. When we are born, we leave the spiritual realm and become individuals. That would be all right if we didn't deny our Source. But inevitably, we do cut off and deny God in various ways and then feel guilty as a result. This is probably the root of the concept of "original sin." We become so engrossed in the physical world that we deny and distort God. However, the spiritual impulse toward wholeness doesn't completely leave us. We yearn for the "oceanic" feeling of unity even as we deny our spirituality. This yearning often leads us further astray.

We often choose what are called, the seven "deadly sins" (anger, sloth, pride, gluttony, envy, lust, greed) because they seem quicker, more attainable and more fun than following a Spiritual path. Then, when "bad" things happen (negative events, circumstances or feelings) we sometimes see these "sins" as punishment from God. Our guilt requires punishment. Actually, the seemingly negative events are results of ego based choices. The fearful ego, chooses these sinful activities which have negative consequences in the long run. Vivid examples are lung cancer caused by years of smoking or a potentially great relationship ruined by angry, ego based misunderstandings. These are not punishments from God; they are results of a fearful ego and negative beliefs. They seem like punishments because we are full of guilt for what we have done. But these outcomes can be used as opportunities to join with the Higher Self to pursue maturity and a better life.

Still, the idea of being punished by God persists. Few people understand what they might have done to deserve such punishment-their guilt is unconscious. Frequently, patients will ask what they did wrong. They also live in fear of what the next punishment will be. The negative events and circumstances seem cruel and unfair. They are unaware that their guilt is related to separation, both at the psychological and Spiritual level. They are also unaware of the long term impact of consciously choosing the quick fixes that have sometimes been called sin. They are unaware of how much their lives would improve if they chose a more spiritual life. They are unaware that interdependence is what is needed, interdependence with family, interdependence with community, and most of all, *interdependence with God*. When we are interdependent with God we let ourselves be guided by the highest principles of love and light. By aligning ourselves with Godly values, our will becomes God's will. This harmony is a result of our choice. We are now co-creators of a more Spiritually aware reality. One might say God's motto is, "I love you. Become your unique self, but always remember your source, and let me guide you."

This is not to say that nothing bad ever happens to Spiritual people. But the more we turn to Spirit for strength and answers, the better we are able to cope with what life gives us and use the process for further growth. For example, Dr. Victor Frankl used his time in a concentration camp to write a book on whatever scraps of paper he could find. This book, *Man's Search For Meaning*, helped millions of people when published after the war. Psychiatrist Roberto Assagioli was also imprisoned during the war and used the time for intense meditation. He remembered his years in prison as some of the best years of his life.

Exaggerated independence is often taught by parents who believe there is no God. These materialists believe their children have to be tough to face a harsh, cruel reality. No matter how tough they are, people who believe in no God or Higher Power at all are prone to anxiety. To such people, the events of life are then random. Anything terrible can happen at any moment for no reason. They often feel alone and isolated in a hostile, uncontrollable world. At best, they heroically face their imminent demise as did existentialists John Paul Sartre and Bertrand Russell. At worst they are plagued by fear and anxiety.

The twin beliefs in separation from a vengeful God and materialism (no God) are truly toxic to both mind and body. Interdependence would be much healthier. Just as the ability to be interdependent with parents and siblings helps us mature psychologically, the ability to be interdependent with God helps us be strong and harmonious. If we have faith that God exists and wants to help us, we can turn to him in prayer and ask for help. It is then up to us to *use* that help to develop our uniqueness and make our social contribution. Why then do so many of us persist in the toxic beliefs of no God or a God that doesn't respond to our needs?

The Guilty Materialist Answer

The most obvious answer is that our *senses* tell us that reality is only that which is material. "I can see, hear, feel and taste something that is real. If I can't sense it physically, it isn't there." This is what Jung called the *sensate* approach to life, gathering information from the senses for survival. But Jung also believed that information that sustained life always had a balancing second source. He called these dual sources of information, "polarities."

The balance for sensation is *intuition*. These two very different ways of gathering information form Jung's first polarity. The sensate approach acknowledges only information gained through the senses. It teaches us that there is nothing but an objective, material reality as perceived by the senses. Such knowledge can then lead us to "logical" conclusions about the world. Such as the thought: If there is nothing but the material, I am my body and I will be extinguished when I die.

Fortunately, the sensate function is balanced by the intuitive function. Intuition is the ability to perceive something all at once, as a whole, without the process of logical deduction or reasoning. Thus, with little logic one can "just know" something. For example, many people intuitively sense there is *something* after physical death. For people who are overbalanced toward logic and reasoning, this is unfathomable. "How can you believe something like that?" they may ask. "I only believe what I see, hear and touch."

The price of this over-reliance on the sensory and rational is *fear*. We fear that the sensory is all there is and that the logical conclusion of obliteration at death is *reality*. In fact, Dr. Ernest Becker, in his book, *The Denial Of Death* felt that death anxiety was the root of *all* psychological problems. Unfortunately, Becker, an anthropologist, completely denied the Spiritual and saw no way out of life's dilemma.

Fortunately, intuition is rarely totally absent. Despite the pull of the senses, something nags at us, telling us there is something more to life than meets the eye. Our intuitive processes are a necessary balance to our sensory knowledge. Intuition, when developed to a high degree can dispel much of our fear. Interestingly, intuition can also help us gain faith. In order to overcome fear, faith must be strengthened and prayer is one way of doing this. Prayer helps us develop our intuition, enabling us to perceive the Godly realms, in ways that can never be realized through the senses and logic.

The Second Polarity

The other polarity described by Jung is thinking and feeling. People who are more oriented toward thinking than feeling tend to deny the unseen, metaphysical world, while people who are more feeling oriented use their kinesthetic feelings to obliquely sense an unseen world in a way unapproachable by logical thought. Our society is prejudiced in favor of logical thinking and sensory gained data. These are the (so called) male ends of the polarities and our society is male dominated. Thus, intuitive, feeling information is often scoffed at by people oriented in the other direction.

A study reported in the New York Times (Nov. 11, 1997) reported the effective use of biofeedback in helping children with attention deficit disorder (A.D.D.). The study showed significant improvement on the part of many children in their ability to pay attention. Perhaps the most interesting part of the article was the reaction of the doubtless sensate, thinking "experts" in the field of A.D.D. These "experts" simply denied the study as inconclusive and unimpressive. They reaffirmed their belief that drugs are the only answer. Their patients therefore will be denied biofeedback help because of their doctor's refusal to balance perceptions. Their "logic" tells them this is a physical disorder which *cannot* be helped by this unproven psychological technique. What a shame that these so called experts are so unbalanced and closed-minded.

One look at most any school system shows the prejudice toward sensory knowledge, logic and thought. Math, science, English, history and language are the "major" subjects. Art, music, drama, dance etc. are the "minor" subjects. Thus, every school child in this country learns early-on what is more important in the culture. Intuition, inspiration, art, music and dance are considered secondary faculties and disciplines.

These are strongly held cultural beliefs, adhered to by most people in our society. Unfortunately, sensory information and logical thought which grows out of sensory information, are exactly the wrong end of each polarity to emphasize if one wants to experience the Spiritual level of life. Senses will tend to reinforce the material nature of life. God cannot be found through logical, rational thought—based on purely sensory information.

Michael Washburn would say that people who are dominated by the senses and linear logic have repressed the unconscious *too well*. They are the people with so called "strong egos." They must become open to *balancing* logic with intuition and feeling if they want to overcome the *fear* imposed by over-reliance on the senses and logic. Faith in a Higher Power can be gained by development of intuition and feeling. Prayer is a means to develop the intuitive and feeling aspects of life.

Faith Isn't Blind

As we open up to intuition and feeling, a new kind of logic emerges. This is a logic based upon the unique beliefs held by each person. Intuition and feelings then become the guides toward a more spiritually based belief system. As a psychotherapist, I have learned that the way to begin helping people is to help them be *aware* of their outmoded or negative beliefs. There is a time of life—young adulthood—when reliance on logic and thinking has value. Young adulthood is the time of establishing oneself in the physical world and our senses and logic help us do that. People who repress Spirituality in favor of strong ego development sometimes do well at first, at least materially. However, the older one gets, the more limited one is by over-reliance on sensory and thinking data. A therapist may help us expand our horizons by empathically pacing and leading our explorations into intuition and feeling. The pace is our own pace, mirrored back to us. The leading is a leading into our own psyche, taking us where is needed to heal, to reach the spiritual level.

In the upcoming section, I will be using words and metaphors to pace and lead you to a position where you can open up to your intuition and feelings. This, in turn enables us to pray for guidance in developing faith in the loving, peaceful essence of the unseen world of the deep unconscious, and to *"hear" the answers.*

Too much reliance on sensory and cognitive information is in itself toxic. But…that is where we must start if we are to build our faith to the level where we *know* (as Jung did) that God exists and wants to help us overcome our fears. Re-education begins at the thinking level, opening up the possibility that there may be something more than just the material world. I include here some basic openings to the intuitive, feeling side of life, followed by some prayers and a self hypnotic induction to help foster the balancing process.

A Metaphor: Have You Ever Seen an Electron?

Almost everyone believes that the material world consists of atoms, which are themselves composed of protons, neutrons and electrons whirling around them. Atomic theory thus tells us that there is more space than solidity in objects. Do you believe this? Why? You see and feel that objects are solid. Have you ever seen an electron? The usual response is that scientists have seen electrons and they have told us that these things exist. Why then, do we believe scientists more than our *senses*? Our eyes tell us that objects are solid. How then can we believe then that there is actually more space than solidity there? We over-rule our senses: "Yes the objects seem material, but we *know* because our high priests, the scientists, tell us that if we look more deeply into matter, there is really more space than our eyes tell us." We acknowledge that our senses are giving us only partial information. For our purposes we treat these objects as solid, even though we know they are really not.

I wonder (paraphrasing Shakespeare) whether there *is* more in Heaven and Earth than we dream of "Horatio." This metaphor tells us that our senses are not necessarily the last word. Perhaps there is more to reality than they can tell us. Perhaps there is an unseen Spiritual world beneath the surface of our physical world. Perhaps this metaphor can help us open up to that world and increase our faith in its beneficial nature.

A Metaphor to Dispel the "Punishing God" Concept

It's cold outside. The wind is howling. But it's a bright sunny winter day. The parent of the four-year-old tells him, "We are going outside, it's cold, let's put on your coat." "No", replies the child, "I don't want to." "Come on now, it's cold out there." the parent replies patiently. "No it's not, it's sunny" replies the child." Now the parent begins to lose her cool. "Just put it on, I'll help you." "No, I won't." A struggle ensues. The child runs outside without a coat, and screams so much his throat becomes sore. The stress is such that the sore throat also becomes infected with strep. The child, who has attended Sunday school asks, "Mommy, why did God give me a sore throat?"

The caring mother explains that God did not give him a sore throat and tells him an infection is causing the hurt. The infection was caused by the stress of screaming followed by the strep bacteria. He isn't ready to understand these concepts yet, but the mother has tried. For the young child, it was more important to get his way, based on his limited knowledge, than to stay well. If he had just listened, he might have avoided the pain. But his mother realizes that he needs to go through some pain in order to learn. She knows that some day he'll be able to accept that sometimes more mature people know better. Sometimes your senses lead you astray. What looks like a warm day is really cold. So she intervenes in a loving way, caring for her son, giving him medicine, explaining that God didn't do it and it isn't *punishment* for his misbehavior. Next time he'll know to put on a coat when it's sunny but cold and not to scream. Perhaps some day he will understand that God does not cause us pain.

Another Metaphor: The Case of the Borderline Patient

People with what people call "borderline unstable personalities" are difficult challenges for all therapists. The disorder is characterized by extreme anger, anxiety, panic, unstable relationships, fears of abandonment, depression, suicidal thoughts, blaming others for their plight, and identity confusion. People with this disorder are so out of control that they are looking for a hero to rescue them. The alleged hero might be a lover, relative or therapist. As long as the hero is sympathetic, nurturant and agrees with their negative view of the world, they are the greatest. As soon as they show some small lack of empathy or disagree with the "victim thinking" and projection of blame onto everyone else, they are villains. Every therapist has endured the wrath of an irate borderline patient, blaming them for some small lack of empathy or not getting better.

Often therapists are seduced emotionally by these patients who, at first praise them. "You are the first therapist (of ten) who understands me. You are wonderful." The experienced therapist takes this in, but knows that there will be an explosion some day. He knows that this patient was deeply wounded by narcissistic, unstable parents. The primary caretakers did not support the child's independence, especially between the ages of 18 to 36 months. The primary caretakers reacted with either too much anxiety or total indifference as the child began to assert her independence. There were too many angry clashes. Often, there was emotional distancing to punish the child. Guilt and fear were used for control. The child learned that the world is a dangerous, hostile, unpredictable, explosive place. That is because her world was that way. She doesn't know what it's like to have loving, mature, consistent parents.

But the child doesn't want to hate her parents, so she covers up her anger at their behavior. Perhaps she alternates between hating them and distancing herself, and needing them so much she clings to them. This is the borderline pattern. They don't know any other way. Later, when others, especially lovers, reject them for their clinginess or aloofness (or both, alternating), they blame the other person. The rage is intense, how can this significant other not *give* them what they need so desperately, stability, security, and self esteem. The confused lover leaves. The patient is devastated.

Enter the experienced therapist. He knows the cause of the person's problems. The patient, however, doesn't really know the cause. And even if she does, has no idea how to get better, other than to find a hero. She is so fragile and upset, all she wants to do is feel better, *now*! The compassionate therapist knows that there will be pain in the therapeutic process. His patient can't get better if he just gratifies all her self-centered needs and agrees with her victim view of the world. She may feel better temporarily but she won't *get* better. Getting better means she will have to go through the pain of maturing beyond her psychic wounds, her victim belief system, her self centered behavior and projection of all responsibility for her life onto others or to bad luck.

The therapist knows that even if he could magically make her feel better, it wouldn't last because she would re-create her distorted relationships again and again. He knows that the only thing he can do is become *a stable loving presence*, always there to listen empathically and support all moves toward a stability that can help her cope with her intense feelings. This stability will take a long time to create. Her negativity, projection of blame, and extreme judgmental nature must gradually be brought to light and transformed. All movements toward mature interdependence must be supported. But she wants a fast magic cure. The therapist patiently practices tolerance, restraint and compassion as she attacks him for being uncaring, incompetent, and not understanding how bad she feels. He does understand. He just knows that a magic cure of symptoms (even if he had one, which he doesn't) would be useless. But he also knows that there is a light at the end of the tunnel. She can be nurtured through her rage and dependency toward the parents. Forgiveness can be achieved after much hard work. Healthy interdependence can gradually be gained with others. Finally, love is available from human beings and the Higher Power. As her relationships improve, she realizes this. The therapist knew what he was doing early on when he didn't "save" her. He had faith in the healing power of God. He can see the overall plan better than the patient. Now, though the patient still has her struggles, she is much better.

Give Us a Hero God

Perhaps we are looking for a heroic God who can save us. If God really knew how bad we felt, wouldn't he do something to save us the pain? What kind of a God would ignore our fervent pleas for help? Does God hate us? Is he punishing us for our bad behavior? Do we deserve this pain? Or perhaps we think there isn't any God. At least then we might see ourselves as victims of bad luck who can end our pain via suicide. Are we all borderline patients, demanding that God save us, make us feel better, demanding that he prove his power now by healing us now, else we deny he has any power?

God's Reply

God, the loving presence in all of us, smiles metaphorically and asks: So how are you feeling today? I am here to listen to you. It's all right to complain. I know you had it rough in childhood. I know it's hard to be you. But when you take responsibility for your current life and turn to me for guidance, you'll begin to feel better, a little more in control. Are you ready for the next step in your growth? Turn toward me now in prayer. Join with me in meditation. It will be hard. I can't do it for you but I'm always here to love and support you. You decide when to take the next step toward responsibility and growth. Develop a daily spiritual practice. Just remember always that you are loved, no matter what you do or how badly you feel. As you turn to me more and more, I'll be better able to help you to help yourself. Pray for an increase in understanding and your faith in me will grow. *I answer all prayers.* Your prayers will be more powerful as you turn to me more and more and learn how to pray, what to pray for, and understand how I work. You will get there. I am sure you will.

Maria's Story: A Life Saved by Faith

Maria was a twenty-six year old married woman who desperately wanted a child and was having trouble conceiving. A religious Catholic, she turned to a priest who specialized in "healing with the holy spirit." To her great surprise, when the priest touched her she fell down. He then told her that she would conceive within a few months. But Maria suffered with Crohn's disease, a severe inflammation of the colon. A few months after the priest's prayer, she became acutely ill with peritonitis. Her white count was thirty, four times the normal count. The infection was spreading all over her body and the doctors told her she was going to die. They asked to tell her parents the bad news but she refused. Her "still small voice" told her she would live. The priest had told her she would have a child. She *knew* she would live. She prayed fervently for faith and strength. The next morning, her white count dropped to seven. The doctors told her the previous test had been mistaken. Amazingly, the MRI showed that the infection had cleared up significantly in other parts of her body. So, they decided to operate; they removed five feet of her bowel. Interestingly, her son was born on 8/8/88 at 8 P.M. with 8 surgeons present after 8 hours of labor. She recovered quickly and three months later she was pregnant!

Does prayer work to increase faith?

Thank you God for opening up my intuition. Or, My intuition is opening up now.

Thank you God for enabling me to open up to my feelings and allowing them to guide me. Or, I am opening up to my feelings and allowing them to guide me.

Prayers can also be more direct. For example;

Thank you God for increasing my faith in the safe and loving nature of the universe. Or, My faith in the safe and loving nature of the universe is increasing.

Prayers can also be aimed at gradually changing toxic beliefs. In regard to faith there is:

Thank you God for helping me see that the world is safer than I thought. Or, the world is safer than I thought.

Later, this can be replaced with:

Thank you God for allowing me to realize I live in a safe universe. Or, I live in a safe universe.

Faith replaces fear. Any prayer affirming faith or reducing fear is good. It is also helpful to meld the intuitive grasp of a new found faith with a conscious logical understanding of *why*, for example, the world is safer than you thought. This can then be followed by the affirmation of help by the Higher Power in changing the negative, toxic beliefs mentioned above, thereby increasing faith. Ultimately you can get to the truth that faith replaces fear.

Self Hypnosis

The self-hypnotic or trance state is ideal for doing the belief changing work necessary to produce spiritual growth. Self-hypnosis is characterized by relaxation, enhanced susceptibility to suggestion, concentration, age regression and re-living of emotions, among many others. Psychologists have known since the time of Mesmer (late 1700s) that trance states were capable of producing healing on both the physical and psychological level. At first, cures were simply suggested and often accomplished via the will power or "animal magnetism" of the hypnotist. However, the "cure" often wore off after a few days because the belief system underlying the illness or psychological problem remained unchanged. Once psychoanalysis was established, however, hypnotherapists quickly caught on to the need for belief change for a more permanent cure. Thus, *hypnoanalysis* was developed.

In brief, hypnoanalysis allows the person to explore the emotionally damaging roots of the problem, producing a sort of catharsis called *abreaction*. This is a releasing of the repressed emotion behind the negative belief, allowing it's replacement with a more positive belief. In fact, Milton Erickson, M.D. founder of modern hypnotherapy once said that "psychotherapy is the replacement of a bad idea with a good idea." Following Erickson's lead, we may say that *faith is a better idea than fear*. Thus, after examining and rooting out fear related beliefs, we may suggest more positive faith enhancing ideas. In short, after proper examination of the existing fear laden beliefs we are implanting prayers as post-hypnotic suggestions. As you will see, the trance helps you contact all levels of your unconscious mind.

The personal unconscious contains the repressed traumatic memories that should be remembered, felt and released. The *superconscious* as described by Jung and Assagioli is the Spiritual level of being. Here, everything is peaceful, loving bliss. It is a state that can be reached when enough psychological work is done. Once it is reached, it can form a sort of backdrop of enlightenment to one's daily activities, a source of guidance and inspiration. One final note: I always use a *permissive* approach of hypnosis and post hypnotic suggestion. I do not want to impose my will on anyone. Thus, I always include the phrase, "if it's all right with your unconscious…"

A Self Hypnotic Trance for Increasing Faith

This section may be used in various ways. It may be read through once as a preliminary but, more importantly, it should be used in conjunction with developing the unconscious and superconscious minds. Thus, you may meditate on it after reading it, or, you may record the trance verbatim in your own voice, speaking slowly, pausing frequently.

Make yourself comfortable and begin to allow your body to relax. Just Follow your breathing…In and Out…Allowing each breath to take you deeper inside yourself. There is nothing that you have to do right now…You are just resting and allowing yourself to move into a state of mind where you are comfortable, calm and relaxed…yet…you are very alert and focused…each breath is making you, at the same time more comfortable and more focused…

Your conscious mind can take a rest now…take all the time you need to let your consciousness become focused and relaxed…allowing your unconscious to emerge…your unconscious has many levels…there is the superconscious, Higher Self…and the personal unconscious with so many memories, feelings and its own belief system…Your unconscious is very alert and it is very obedient and acts according to it's beliefs...and you have a belief system, just as surely as you have a digestive, circulatory and nervous system...and your unconscious creates your reality according to your beliefs...

Are you ready to let go of one of your old dysfunctional or negative beliefs? Would you like to let go of your belief in fear??? Once you are focused on which belief you need to change...you can tap into the personal area of your unconscious...you can see in images, words, feelings how that belief was created...You can feel the emotions holding that belief in place...it is safe now to really feel the fear...and if it's all right with your unconscious...you are able to let the intense belief in fear dissipate,...creating the possibility of newer more functional, spiritual beliefs to take their place...

Your spiritual self, your Higher Self knows that you are safe...Is your lower unconscious ready to realize that you live in a safe universe?. As soon as your lower unconscious lets go of it's belief in fear, your fear is gone....Now, there is a source of power that can change your negative beliefs for you...the power resides in a deeper level of your unconscious...a place where all is harmonious, peaceful and loving...some people call this the Higher Self....others call it God...still others call it the Ground of Being...but it is a Higher Power and it has the power to help that lower unconscious part of You to release it's old belief in fear and separation...the Higher Self has the power to heal fear through faith and love...are you ready to turn to this Higher Power within for your healing?

If you need more time to process your feelings...take the time you need...you can continue to process the feelings while you go about your daily activities, while you sleep, until you are ready to thank God for allowing faith, powered by universal unconditional love, to replace fear...In fact from now on...each time you are afraid you will find yourself thanking God for increasing your faith...the fear will ebb away until it vanishes completely...your faith is becoming stronger and stronger each time you face fear and replace it with a calm assurance that your Higher Self, your loving Higher Power, God, is guiding you into situations designed to increase your faith.

You are in an alliance with your Higher Self now...Your life is going exactly as planned by God...You are now cooperating with the spiritual learning process...and the more you cooperate...the stronger your faith becomes...you are beginning to feel the deep joy of faith, trust, allowing the deepest spiritual level of the unconscious run your life...using your conscious mind to make the choice of faith over fear, again and again until it becomes automatic...

Notice how you are calmer now...how your life works better now. You can use this process as many times as you wish...The more fearful experiences you let go of, the more your faith increases...feel how good it feels in your body, to have faith in the Higher Power...to join and cooperate with the Higher Self...and the prayer: Thank you God for replacing my fear with faith helps you every day of your life...at some point you will notice that your life has become a prayer...

Now whenever your conscious mind is ready to cooperate with your unconscious in increasing your faith, your eyes will open and you will feel so much better than you did before...that's right allow your eyes to open, feeling good.

Utilization of this trance helps you focus inward. It enables you to use both levels of the unconscious, the personal and the transpersonal. At the personal level, it is helpful to re-experience any traumas that are being held onto or used as an excuse for not forming a Spiritual Alliance with the Higher Self. At the personal level, it is as if your ego is saying, "I won't be happy until you apologize for treating me badly in childhood." Since you can't go back and change childhood, then you would never be happy. Fortunately, there is a deeper, more powerful level of Being which we are calling the Higher Self. This Godly level of the unconscious can overrule the puny ego level but only if it is reached, experienced and appealed to. This, hypnotic trance enables you to reach, experience and appeal to the Godly level of the unconscious. This particular trance deals with increasing faith. In later chapters, trances will deal with increasing strength, love and forgiveness.

CHAPTER SIX

MOVING BEYOND INFERIORITY

The inferiority complex is so common that were it considered an illness, it would be an epidemic. Jung defined a complex as a constellation of ideas related to a *perceived* failure. The idea that we are not "good enough" defines the inferiority complex. Let us pursue this idea a bit further. We may ask, "not good enough for what?" The obvious answer is, not good enough to please our significant others, parents at first. Later, it's not good enough to compete with our peers in whatever areas we deem important. At least in the United States (and probably western Europe as well), we live in a culture of achievement. We are as good as what we do and how well we do it. This leads to constant comparison with others and frequently coming up with the idea that we are falling short. You might think that this only applies to the "losers" of the world and that successful people think they are good enough. This is simply not the case.

I was a good student who frequently got "could do better" checked off on my report card. I was then exhorted by my parents to try harder. Since I felt like I was trying, my conclusion was that I "wasn't good enough." In the ninth grade I had a good year, 89.8 average. I was feeling good. Then I overheard my father say, "You know, he's almost a genius." That was it. I sank into despair. I knew I would never be a genius. Even at fourteen, I already felt I was not good enough. In fact, I felt I was no good at all, since only *genius* was acceptable. Not surprisingly, the next time I got good grades was in graduate school. It was only through many years of therapy, practicing psychotherapy and eventually praying, that I realized I *was* good enough, even if I wasn't a genius. The solution was not to achieve more, but to become spiritually enlightened. We are all good enough because we are all part of God. We are all individualizations of the Ground of Being.

Dr. Karen Horney, in her book *Neurosis And Human Growth*, wrote extensively about the "imposter" syndrome. This is exhibited by successful people, often professionals, who feel that they got through by bluffing or luck. At any moment, they might be found out and completely discredited. I have had many patients with this syndrome. Psychologically, it can always be traced back to their parents being too self-absorbed and narcissistic to give them the love they needed to develop a strong sense of themselves as valuable people. But the real problem is that they have cut off Spirit in favor of joining the competitive world where no amount of success is ever satisfying. Psychotherapy helps many people to gain strength through a positive therapeutic alliance. It feels good to be listened to and "mirrored" by a caring person. However, this psychological work is not a complete answer. In fact, if it is clung to for too long, even good psychological work can be an obstacle to the real answer.

Michael Washburn advises us to start meditating in mid life. He calls this regression in the service of transcendence. He is right, we must eventually turn to the Higher Power-that deeper spiritual level which must be addressed. *A Course In Miracles* tells us that the separation from God is what really causes this sense of inferiority, as well as guilt.

To many people, even those who study *A Course in Miracles*, the Spiritual cause of guilt and inferiority defies "common sense." Now, common sense tells us that once we are born into the world, we are separate. Gradually, we come to believe that we are separate, physically and psychologically. This idea is much more toxic than it seems because it cuts us off from Spirit. What we don't understand is that simultaneously with our physical separation, there is a deeper Spiritual level at which we are not separate at all. *This deeper knowledge will help us to realize that we are not inferior because we cannot be inferior. We are all just part of the Oneness, temporarily in a physical body.* The *Course* urges us to realize this and turn to the Higher Power (Holy Spirit) for guidance. Only by realizing the essential oneness of all things can we live peacefully together on Earth.

In Vedantic Hinduism, this concept is called *maya*. The physical world is a kind of illusion or maya. In reality we are all *atman* (individualized souls) which are actually part of or identical with *Brahma* (God). The people who fully realize this are enlightened and no longer need to reincarnate after bodily death. In other words, the purpose of life in Vedantic Hinduism is to reach this knowledge. You are just as good as anyone else because you are, at the deepest level, the same as them. When you realize this, you become a basically kind, loving, peaceful person who is able to deal well with inevitable misfortune because you know that at another higher level, *it isn't real.* You still feel pain and compassion for others because almost everyone else buys the illusion. That is very sad. In fact it is a major impediment to understanding this concept. It is hard to buck such a consensus belief. Only by prayer, meditation and the experience of oneness can this knowledge be gained. *You are good enough because you are, in essence, God (at your deepest level).*

The Case of the Reluctant Psychologist

Rachel was as 35-year-old school psychologist who had her masters degree. Her presenting problem was a complete inability to work on or hand in her doctoral proposal. Every time she tried she became paralyzed by a sense of anxiety and dread. She was absolutely hopeless about moving ahead. Finally, the anxiety was so bad she couldn't even sleep. She had read my first book, *When Therapy Isn't Enough: The Healing Power Of Prayer and Psychotherapy*, and thought that a spiritual-psychological approach might help.

Her background revealed that she had been an excellent student all the way through school. Yet, she was never "good enough" for her parents, especially her tyrannical father who had always told her that 98 percent was not good enough on an exam, she needed to get 100 percent. Coming from a Hispanic background, she was expected to bring honor to her people and achieve very highly. She was also expected to do a significant amount of housework and be like a second mother to younger siblings. She took on too much, too fast. Despite her extreme intelligence, she was unable to appreciate how she put herself through school with little or no familial support. She felt like Horney's imposter who could be exposed at any moment. Further achievement, rather than making her feel good, seemed likely to make her feel more responsible and vulnerable to the exposure of her (false) idea that she was not good enough.

These realizations in therapy were helpful but she was anxious to implement prayer as well. Her prayers that she is *just as good as anyone else*, were recited in Spanish, her prayer language. This is a good example of Dr. Herb Benson's belief that prayer should include meaningful elements for each person. I believe that using Spanish, the language of her youth, made the prayers most effective, since the damage was done in her youth. In order to facilitate the prayers still further, hypnotic trance was used, with post-hypnotic suggestions for additional prayers included. She now thanks God daily for enabling her to see the Spiritual truth that she has the power to move ahead in her profession without feeling burdened by the responsibility. The advanced degree would only be a burden if she feels like an incompetent fraud. She no longer feels burdened by the idea of her doctorate. The more she prays, the more she has been able to write. She handed in her proposal, a triumph in itself. Her proposal was accepted and the rest of her thesis is being written. She feels hopeful of getting her degree within the year.

The Case of the Dependent Wife

Maggie was a fifty-four-year old housewife, complaining of depression and agoraphobia-fear of going too far from home and getting a panic attack. She was unable to work or drive due to her fear of panic attacks. She was entirely dependent on her husband for any mobility or social life. She also was deeply resentful of this dependency, yet was unable to break away. She had no income or means of support other than her husband. He was a deeply depressed, angry man himself who was wholly unwilling to examine his emotions or get any help. Instead, he blamed her for his problems. He criticized her harshly for being a spendthrift, and generally incompetent person. Understandably, she felt totally trapped and hopeless.

Her background revealed that her father had treated her much the same way as her husband had. She had constantly been told she was dumb and incompetent and the only thing she could do would be to get married and have a family. She never went to college, married young and had two children. Early in her marriage, she developed agoraphobia with panic attacks. In her own words, she "was afraid of everything." Eventually she got very depressed about this condition as well as her deteriorating marriage. She had received previous therapy which had been somewhat helpful, but she felt that she could never be happy living with her husband although she felt she was too weak and useless to leave him.

She came to me depressed, anxious and hopeless with no idea how to help her situation. At first glance she seemed almost as hopeless as she was presenting herself. Fortunately, we soon discovered that she did have a strong belief in God. Raised as a Catholic, she felt certain that there is a powerful God whom she had certainly displeased. She felt like she was a "good person" who was being punished for crimes she didn't understand.

The idea of prayer appealed to her. She said that she did pray often, but that her prayers were scattered and never answered. After all, she was still miserable, phobic and stuck in her awful marriage. The first step for her was to change the *way* she was praying. She was taught how to use prayers of thankfulness. Such prayers assume that the prayer has already been answered. She thanked God for giving her strength. She thanked God for helping her see things differently. Then she needed to develop patience to see the differences in her life. She began to affirm daily that she was just as good as anyone else. She improved in fits and starts. Sometimes she felt more hopeful. Other times she felt more discouraged than ever.

At some point, she began to improve and decided that she would look for "mini-miracles." She still yearned for a hero God who would rescue her with one big miracle. But she began to notice that her life was better in small ways. She enjoyed her grandchildren more. She enjoyed her dog more. She got out more and ventured further from her home. She even went driving a few times. In short, she began to come out of her depression and experience pleasure again. Yet, she was still dissatisfied and felt that she was being punished by God and didn't know what she had done wrong.

The second step in her therapy was for her to see how she was co-creating her reality with God. Gradually, I was able to help her see that God is not vengeful. She was not being punished in any way. Rather, she was merely reaping the results of her negative belief system and fearful ego. Her beliefs and fears had produced negative thoughts: angry, vengeful and depressed feelings about herself and her husband. Eventually these negative thoughts had produced her self proclaimed "punishment" (her symptoms), which she thought were being dealt out by God. My analogy was that she was ordering "liver" (her least favorite food). Then when the liver arrived, she was surprised and felt it was a punishment. "Where was the punishment?", I asked, "You ordered the liver." Somehow, this analogy penetrated her defenses and she began to feel and behave differently. Though nothing has overtly changed in her situation, she is feeling differently about it. (The *Course* says that this is the first step in changes of circumstances). Her perception had changed. Her relationship with her difficult adult son had improved significantly. She even noticed small differences in her relationship with her husband.

The primary change in Maggie's situation is that she is no longer praying for *him* to change. She herself is changing by perceiving things differently, and by assuming a different attitude. Her prayers are being answered by the mini-miracles of improved relationships and feelings, due to her changed perceptions. There is still much work ahead. There will be times of discouragement. But she is moving in a positive direction.

Beyond Success and Failure

These two cases show the relative lack of importance of success and failure. Though Rachel had achieved more than Maggie at a younger age, she didn't feel good about herself. Both women needed to realize at an experiential level that they are all right and good enough just the way they are. Although we live in a "bottom line" culture, it is quite possible to be peaceful and happy at any level of so-called success. Just a quick glance at the lives of celebrities tells us that money and fame do not often bring happiness. A successful man like President Kennedy is now being portrayed as a deeply flawed man who was a womanizer and amphetamine addict. The successful basketball player, Latrell Sprewell punched out his coach and lost his 23 million dollar contract. Obviously, the money wasn't making him happy. He internalized the coach's criticism to such a degree that he exploded in rage. Did either of these widely disparate men realize that they were O.K. without super achievement? Obviously not. Was Mother Teresa worried about her bank account, or her next contract or if she had enough money for her old age? No, but most of us worry about these things. If we realize we are just as good as anybody else, we can take criticism. If we are just as good as anyone else we have no big stake in what others think of us. We have no ideal image. We just are, whoever we are.

Philosopher David Spangler was often asked by his students what their unique destiny was. Spangler, who had considerable psychic ability would look and see *absolutely nothing*. His interpretation was that most of us are not destined to be famous or rich. It is *enough* to just use the talents we have and be ourselves. We can be quiet role models to others without preaching anything. In fact, we need to be role models for others. That helps others more than preaching.

It is a common New Age misconception that once we are on the spiritual path we can easily become wealthy, famous, or anything else we have always wanted to be. This is like turning a two year old loose in a candy store. He thinks he knows what he wants, unlimited candy forever. That is why his parents give him limits. God wants us on the Spiritual path, but not so we can let our egos go wild with material glee. Material wealth may or may not be part of our spiritual path.

A Course In Miracles says that all things are lessons God would have us learn. Thus, an important realization on the Spiritual path is that we are just as good as everyone else. This does not mean we have the same gifts, talents or destinies. It means we are all part of the greater whole. Anyone who really knows and experiences this does not feel inferior. We don't need to be famous unless its part of what we have to do here. We can just as well be happy and peaceful with whatever we have right now. It is all in our attitude. Victor Frankl used his good attitude to survive a concentration camp. Latrell Sprewell used his bad attitude to mess up a 23 million dollar contract. Once you really get the spiritual idea that there are no inferior people (only inferior attitudes) you can accept your life as it is. If it is supposed to change in some material way, it will. If it is supposed to change in an attitudinal way, it will. The latter is more important than the former. The Beatles said it well: "Let it be."

Dr. Wayne Dyer on Spirituality

Best selling author and psychologist Wayne Dyer has, over the past twenty years, evolved in a Spiritual direction. In his latest book, *Your Sacred Self*, Dyer teaches us to slow down and appreciate the quiet moments in life. He feels that most people today are too busy trying to overcome inferiority feelings. He recommends saying "no" to over-work and setting aside quiet time each day for prayer, meditation and contemplation of nature. This will help us realize our essential oneness and see the ludicrous nature of inferiority feelings. Dyer is not recom-mending completely dropping out. He is helping other "driven" (by inferiority feelings) people to slow down and just be. At first, this is hard to do. Later, as prayer becomes a regular daily practice, it becomes easier and easier. The essence of inner peace is learning to cooperate with one's Higher Power.

Sometimes, driven, anxious people will complain that if they get too peaceful, life will become boring and unproductive. I have found the reverse to be true. When I am peaceful, I am more able to be produc-tive and enjoy life's processes, including the quiet moments. I have found the same to be true of my patients as they begin to release infe-riority feelings and embrace oneness.

Hypnotic Trance to Heal Inferiority

Hypnotic trance is another excellent vehicle to let go of inferiority feelings and the driven, too busy life that can evolve out of them. Almost all patients report an increase in inner peace after hypnosis.

When this is accompanied by post-hypnotic suggestions for prayers of oneness, the effect is even more pronounced. The following trance may once again be recorded in your own voice and replayed daily. Remember to speak slowly, with frequent pauses. This allows the unconscious to search for information, traumas and solutions at the appropriate points.

Just sit back in your chair and begin to allow your body to relax...Follow your breathing, in and out, in and out...notice subtle feelings, actually feel the air going in...and out...of your lungs...and with each breath you are becoming more relaxed and comfortable...that's right...more comfortable...Yet, part of you is quite alert...hearing every word that I'm saying...and there is no need to do anything now...it is enough to just be here...in this room...comfortable...calm...at peace...your conscious mind can just rest now...all is well...

You can hear without listening. the deepest part of your unconscious hears without listening...it is so easy to just be...in touch with your deep unconscious, your Higher Self...it is your natural state...your birthright that was long ago forgotten...but you remember now...and that brings great peace...you can memorize these peaceful feelings...you can recall these calm feelings at any time...simply by repeating the words deep peace...that's right...deep peace...and you can have an image that goes with the words...you can go anywhere you want...to your own personal peaceful place...see every detail....the more you see, hear, smell, feel...the better it is...this image will also bring you peace...there is no need to strive now...just be, peaceful, in your peaceful place...and there is a reason you lost these comfortable feelings that you have regained now...

You thought you weren't good enough...and you can go back now and see how this false belief got started...take all the time you need to see some childhood events that made you feel inferior...it's O.K. to feel the feelings if you wish...or its O.K. to just see the scenes. whatever would be more helpful...and when you have seen enough...you can let go of those old, inaccurate inferiority feelings...I wonder if you are ready to let go of those feelings now?

If you are not you can continue to review them later as you go about your normal tasks...and while you sleep tonight...until you are ready to let go and see that you are just as good as anyone else...so there is no need to drive yourself harder and harder...it's fine to spend some of your time just relaxing...and there is a reason for this...you are just as good as anyone else because at the deepest level, you are connected to everyone else...you can picture this now and feel this peace now by going deeper into your unconscious...reaching the super conscious mind, the Higher Self...a level of mind where you can see, and feel the interconnectedness of all people...and all things, where all is one...you can experience this oneness now, and...memorize this feeling...allow it to motivate you...allow it to remove the driven feelings...allow true productivity to arise...balanced by periods of meditation and prayer...

Each time you eat a meal...you will remember these peaceful feelings...you will remember to thank the Higher Power...however, you conceive it, for giving you the experience of peace...the knowledge of oneness.......the thankful prayer for oneness will bring you here anytime that is appropriate...simply be thinking the prayer, "thank you for the inner peace I am experiencing...thank you for letting me experience and be motivated by the peace and oneness of the spiritual realm....and whenever you have these prayers and feelings memorized you will be able to open your eyes...come back to the room...feeling good...remembering what you need to remember and forgetting what you need to forget...

You will listen to this tape daily as long as you need it...but never in a car...waiting until you are fully alert before driving or crossing a street...opening your eyes now...coming back to the room...feeling good.

To recapitulate my main points of this chapter: inferiority feelings are rampant due to a lack of spiritual understanding. Very few people realize that they are driven by inferiority feelings. Within our culture, it seems normal to be driven toward success and getting ahead. People who feel that they are on the bottom want to learn how to be on the top. So called "losers" want to be "winners." People who are doing well materially usually think they need to do still better. Very few people are happy and satisfied. The reason for all this unhappiness is that they are looking at life from the point of view of the personal ego. That is, they are identifying totally with a very small part of themselves. The judging ego is not the true self, Karen Horney's idealized image. This puffed up false self is always trying to look good in comparison to others. It is the first to be hurt, disappointed or scornful with others. It seeks to build itself up by tearing others down. It fears low self-esteem and hungers for high self-esteem.

By contrast, the real Self is the Higher Self. This is the Spiritual part, the silent loving presence, the "watcher" who knows that all is really well, deep down. This Godly part of ourselves does not judge or condemn. It does not compare and contrast. It does not manipulate. It does not seek outside approval. It just knows the truth, that there is no such thing as inferiority in the world of Spirit. Most people have not experienced this level yet. Many people deny it even exists. It can only be reached by working with the unconscious, unseen world of spirit, until you can choose to join with the Higher Self in peace. I suggest that no matter what your beliefs in this regard, you suspend them and playfully experiment. Through prayer, meditation, and hypnosis, most people can reach the unconscious.

First, work with the personal unconscious. This aids many people to freely choose peace. Then, move deeper into the spiritual or transpersonal aspect of the unconscious. Most people see results by experiencing the peace. Patience, diligence and support help us to stay on the path. Spirituality is really the best way to lessen and eventually remove inferiority feelings.

If you think you are superior, for any reason, you need more work. Many Spiritual seekers feel hubris or false pride because they are more Spiritual than others. This inevitably leads to further problems. A strong sense of humility is always a component of really getting the point that we are all part of the same oneness. Thank God for helping you see, feel and experience this oneness in a way that appeals to you. Follow your own intuition as to what steps to take to *feel* the Spiritual presence. It doesn't have to be dramatic, but you will know the true sense of peace when it appears. Peace is the product of daily application of the spiritual antidotes to fear, hate, guilt and inferiority. Let us go on now to what is perhaps the hardest quality to develop, forgiveness.

Chapter Seven

How To Forgive Your Enemies

Forgiveness is a way of life. It is an attitude that conflicts violently with what is taught in our society. Although we may pay lip service to the idea of forgiving others, when it comes right down to it we frequently want revenge and justice when we are hurt. The issue of revenge vs. forgiveness comes up in virtually every patient's psychotherapy. All of us have been hurt in one way or another in life. Thus, we must decide how to deal with it. Frequently, we try to avoid the issue by repressing our anger or not thinking about it. Then, it comes out in some backhanded way like panic attacks or physical illness. I have never seen a person with panic attacks that did not have major issues with anger and fear. Yet, without therapy, the connection between fear and forgiveness is rarely made. To most of my patients, the idea of forgiving others seems to have no connection to their symptom. Forgiveness is not seen as a path to peace, but it is.

Some people are aware of their anger and resentment at others, but are completely unwilling to forgive them. Their attitude is, "Why should I let him get away with it?" They want the other person to suffer as they have suffered, preferably even more than they suffered. At the very least, they want the other person to acknowledge their hurtful actions and apologize. The object of revenge isn't to get even, it is to win.

Still other times, people come in all too willing to forgive. At the first session they state that they know their parents did the best they could. So, they have forgiven them. This is premature confession. They are avoiding the real pain of their childhood traumas by pretending to forgive. True forgiveness involves several steps; admitting the hurts, feeling the pain, understanding where the other people were coming from, then gaining strength and self confidence, seeing the problem from another perspective (re-framing), finally forgiving the other and forgiving yourself.

It Was That Bad: Admitting the Hurt

It is amazing how many troubled people try to minimize the agony they have gone through. Even in the safety and comfort of a psychologist's office, they try to minimize the pain they have gone through. This is especially true of wounds from parents, though it certainly holds true for spouses and significant others. It is impossible to truly forgive anyone unless you admit that something went wrong.

In general, what was amiss is that we were raised without enough compassion by people who were too wrapped up in their own troubles to give the unconditional positive regard we all need. Perhaps, you recoiled in fear and shut yourself off from the anger of retribution and punishment. Shutting yourself off from bad feelings alienates you from your unconscious and in some cases all feelings. The Godly part of your unconscious may have been shut off along with the repressed memories in your personal unconscious. Thus, you felt alone and isolated in a harsh world.

Somehow, however, there is a vague sense of guilt about all this. You aren't really sure what the guilt is about. It just feels like is that there is something wrong. Rarely will it ever occur to anyone that what is amiss is that they are cut off from their feelings and from God. That would be tantamount to believing that the entire neurotic system of fear and layers of defense—our very feelings are wrong. Instead we weave tangled webs denying our fear, anger, guilt, resentment and deceit. We convince ourselves that our egoic prison must be defended at all costs from the dangerous outside world. We convince ourselves that only this difficult material world is real and the best we can do is make ourselves comfortable within it. The more we were hurt, the angrier we are.

The only solution seems to be defense, revenge and denial of our feelings and anything beyond the physical observable world. The anger, hate, guilt and fear harbored in the unconscious are too much to face. We think we must deny, repress, project and intellectualize such feelings to get them under control. In order to gain control over these feelings about significant others as well as ourselves, we repress the entire unconscious. In order to become unaware of our true feelings about others in the world we repress both the lower unconscious (where personal feelings and memories reside) and the superconscious (where God resides). This creates a separation from God, which is the biggest tragedy of all. Fortunately, there is a solution to the vague guilt that nags at us. It is a spiritual solution, God's solution, *forgiveness*.

Forgiveness is an important part of the path to true peace. However, to most people, there seems to be too much danger in these powerful feelings (guilt, fear, anger) to even think of forgiving. To most of us, forgiveness just means that the bastards got away with it. We are too cut off from God to even consider the reconciliation of forgiveness.

Robin Casarjian, in her enlightening book, *Forgiveness: A Bold Choice For A Peaceful Heart*, has many suggestions to help people get on the path of forgiveness. She notes that many people are just not ready to forgive those who hurt them the most. In this light, she suggests that her readers begin to forgive on neutral ground. That is, she has them first replace their usual judgmental thoughts about *strangers* with positive loving thoughts. She presents the idea that instead of thinking ill of these strangers, we can remember that they are all part of the greater humanity, and as such are part of God. This is often easier to do than to forgive those closest to us, who have really hurt us. The benefit is that we begin to undo the harmful defense system we have erected to protect our fragile egos (false selves). We tend to judge others relative to what we don't like about ourselves. If we fear getting fat, we may dislike any fat person. If we don't like quiet people, we may dislike anyone who is shy, and so on. This exercise helps us see that whatever we don't like about ourselves we project onto others. When we refuse to judge and instead forgive others, we are forgiving ourselves.

Feeling the Pain

Alice Miller, in her many books including, *The Drama of The Gifted Child, For Your Own Good, and Breaking Down The Wall of Silence*, exposes the cover-up of childhood pain. Miller's main hypothesis is that parents inflict both physical and emotional abuse on their children, thinking it's "for their own good." In actuality, they are displacing the brutality that was done to them by their parents and others onto their own children. Thus, generation after generation of abused children keep the cycle going. The repressed, denied and projected feelings of anger, fear, and guilt continue to cause individual misery and world-wide chaos. Miller's solution is to admit that "it really was that bad", and allow yourself to acknowledge the feelings that were too painful and dangerous to feel in childhood.

Miller believes that forgiveness arises naturally once you have admitted how bad things were in your childhood and allow yourself to feel the pain and grieve for the unconditional acceptance you didn't get. You cannot go back and get that kind of love from other people now that you are an adult. But you can forgive, and unconditionally accept yourself. This process will re-awaken all the feelings that have lied dormant while you were emotionally frozen in defense of your fragile ego. As the process continues, it becomes more possible to interact with the Spiritual side of yourself. This Spiritual side will then aid you in continuing this growth process. Thus, allowing yourself to feel the pain leads to forgiveness, which opens you up to the tender side of yourself that you have long buried. This newfound tenderness may lead you toward a new understanding of the other and why he or she hurt you. You can now see that it had little or nothing to do with you. You are now able to give and accept love, due to your willingness to forgive others and yourself.

A brief prayer will help: *Thank You God for helping me to see that my parents were too damaged themselves to show me the love I needed. I forgive them. I forgive myself.*

Why Your Parents Didn't Love You Unconditionally

Under ideal conditions all parents would love their children unconditionally. Unfortunately, this is the exception. Most people are so caught up in their own neurotic need to be loved enough, good enough or successful enough, they don't have unconditional regard for their offspring. Some may love helpless babies but become more critical later. Others may hate helpless babies (hating their own helplessness) and gradually accept a more mature child. At every step of the way, as parents, there are new needs of the child that must be recognized and dealt with. Unfortunately, each stage *unconsciously reminds* the parents of their own issues at that stage. Then, not wanting to remember the pain, the parent reacts harshly toward the confused child. Further pain ensues, painful emotions are aroused, defenses are erected in the children and the process continues.

In the process of psychotherapy, the person is encouraged to remember the hurts. This helps because it releases energy and paves the way to forgiveness. But sometimes the process omits understanding the hurts of the parents as *they* grew up with their self-centered parents. Understanding can lead to true forgiveness.

I have sometimes joked that my problems started in 1921. People look at me blankly, knowing I'm not that old. Then I tell them that was the year *my mother* was a two-year old. I picture my grandparents mishandling my mother at that time, which led to her rage which she later directed toward me. This imagery process helps me to forgive and love my mother.

A good exercise to practice is imagining your mother or father as a child, being dealt with uncompassionately by their parents. This helps you to see that your parents have unconsciously acted out their feelings on you. They were hurt too.

A brief prayer can help again: *Thank you God for helping me see that my parents were just doing to me what they were programmed to do. It had nothing to do with me. They were just projecting their feelings toward their parents onto me.*

Feeling Strength from Forgiveness

It is interesting to feel how you gain strength from being more forgiving. A tremendous amount of energy is wasted defending yourself against fear, anger, resentment, guilt and other emotions. The energy is spent repressing fear that these emotions might emerge and be experienced. Once you allow them to be experienced and forgive your tormentors there is nothing left to fear. You are now free to forgive (though you won't forget), and to use your energy to help others.

Those early hurts and rejections may seem to be the only cause of your latent inferiority feelings. You thought you were bad or not good enough because of the cruel way others reacted to you. Actually, these hurts were only part of it. In pushing away your hurt feelings, you also pushed away God. And *that* is the biggest problem. *With the release forgiveness brings*, you realize that they were just acting out their feelings. They also shut off their hurt feelings and shut out God. It had nothing to do with you. You actually were and *are* good enough. You are good enough because you are part of the oneness of God. You are a holy child of God. Your natural feelings are good. It is right to feel happy and energized. As one patient put it, "I feel *good*. Is this the way you are supposed to feel?, This is unbelievable." He was feeling the energy that was released as he began to forgive his bosses, his parents, and ultimately himself.

A brief prayer: *Thank You God for helping me see that I am good enough, my feelings are good, I am just as good as anyone else.*

Reframe Your Life through Forgiveness

You cannot consciously choose the events of your life, but you can always choose your attitude toward them. A forgiving attitude paves the way for a Spiritual outlook on life. This means that events are looked at as challenges rather than insurmountable obstacles. It means that hidden within even the most dire happenings are the seeds of Spiritual awakening. A serious illness can lead to the blossoming of mature love. An earthquake can lead to selfless devotion to helping injured victims. Internment in a concentration camp can lead to writing books on the importance of meaning (Dr. Victor Frankl) or the superconscious mind (Dr. Roberto Assagioli). The overall goal is to stop blaming others as the reason you *can't* do this or that. Instead you can look at others as characters within the play that you are writing. Your (so called) enemies were put there to challenge you to develop all the positive Spiritual qualities you can. You are supposed to be working on becoming more loving, forgiving, kind, non-judgmental, faithful etc. If you didn't run into problems you wouldn't be able to develop fully as a Spiritual being.

A Course in Miracles advocates this reframing method, telling us that the only purpose of life is to join with others in forgiveness and prayers for guidance. This enables us to perceive the true oneness of all creation. At the human level it helps us solve problems by seeing things differently. All we really need to do, says *The Course*, is to go outside the ego system and ask the Higher Power for a way to see things in terms of a "win-win" situation. Gradually, we learn to choose peace instead of insisting on ego goals like being right, winning, or getting revenge. Only the Higher Power can give us the strength and insight to make the obvious choice of peace. The ego will always encourage us to compete, win, take revenge and pursue some perceived absolute justice. Thus, the ego is the enemy of peace.

We must forgive ourselves and others in order to find peace. Realization of the true oneness of all creation is behind the idea of forgiveness. We forgive not because we are condescendingly superior, but because we are all part of the same source and are therefore guiltless and blameless. If we continue to follow the egoic path, we will continue to suffer as we have for thousands of years. If we appeal to the Higher Power in prayer, and follow the path of forgiveness, we will develop a sense of peace and strength.

Forgiving Others

We are still left with the problem of justice. How can we let those bastards get away with what they did? From the ego's point of view, the idea of retributive justice makes sense: we cannot let those who hurt us get away with anything. "If we give them an inch, they'll take a mile." This holds true as long as everyone is thinking on the ego's level. However, there is another level-the spiritual dimension. Here, everything is different, miracles do occur, pointing the way to a new, forgiving world.

Psychologist Carolyn Miller, in her book, *Creating Miracles: Understanding the Experience of Divine Intervention*, recounts many stories of people who found themselves in dire, life threatening situations. Instead of responding with fear, anger, hate, and struggle, they responded with calm acceptance, peace and forgiveness. The result was invariably a miraculous rescue or recovery.

For example, Miller tells the story of a woman who was approached by two men on a dark street near her beach home. When they threatened to rape her, she had an unusual reaction. Rather than getting angry or afraid, she surrendered to the awful situation. Her thought was that as awful as rape was, it would be even more awful in a gravel parking lot. She suggested to them that they come with her to her apartment so she wouldn't rip her new dress. Her accepting, paradoxical attitude confused them but they followed her. On the way home, talked to them in such a calm manner that they decided not to rape her. Instead, they admonished her to be very careful out in the world, as everyone was not as nice as they.

Miller concludes that a surrendering, accepting attitude actually changes the circumstances of any situation. The victim's calm acceptance took her right out of the attacker-victim dyad. When faced with acceptance instead of fear and anger, the rapists changed their attitude and let her go. Rape is not about sex, it is about fear and power.

This is only one of many examples Miller gives. In each case, however, the "victim" changes the eventual outcome via a surrendering, accepting, forgiving, peaceful attitude. Am I suggesting that all rape victims just submit to their attackers? No. A careful study of Miller's cases suggest that the key element in transforming the situations is lack of fear. Rapists thrive on fear. They are intimidators because they themselves were once brutally intimidated. In psychology we call this "identification with the aggressor." Rapists have something in common with dictators. Hitler, for example, was brutally beaten by his father. He learned to laugh at the beatings and took his pain out on the whole world. Rapists have internalized their brutal tormentors and are acting out their rage on others who they want to fear them. In the examples Miller presents, the victims surrendered to what seemingly was going to inevitably happen. This made them relax and confused the attackers who expect fear and struggle. The result was the termination of the attacks.

It remains to be seen how widespread the effects of such an attitudinal shift might be. What is clear is that anger and fear do not help people survive dire situations. Forgiving an aggressor does not mean you condone his actions though. The medieval Jewish philosopher Moses Maimonides suggested that you must tell the person who hurt you what they have done. If you do not do this, *you* become the "sinner." What this means is that the smoldering resentment in you makes you miss the spiritual mark. You can strongly express and assert your rights along with forgiveness. This is your part in the process. You may hope for an apology and a change in attitude on the part of the wrong doer but you can't control others. They may be clueless, and never understand how they hurt you. In cases with people you actually know, your job is to tell them how they hurt you in the past, set limits on the unacceptable behavior and then forgive them. In cases involving serious crimes like rape, you undoubtedly have to go through the rage and grief described earlier. Only then could you possibly develop real forgiveness. A different, more forgiving, peaceful yet assertive attitude toward wrongdoers will help bring you and the world toward peace and harmony.

Forgiving Yourself

Forgiving yourself could be the most important form of forgiveness. How many people do you know who are too hard on themselves? Are you too hard on yourself? Do you find it hard to let go of guilt for past misdeeds or omissions? If so, you might be a victim of what Dr. Karen

Horney calls "unconscious self hate." Such self deprecation can take many forms. It can appear as panic attacks, depression, physical illness or generalized anxiety and fatigue.

Self hate is based upon the ideas that we are not good enough, or that we have done something wrong. Thus, we attack ourselves, sometimes unmercifully, as punishment. In doing so we are *both* the sadist and the masochist, the torturer and the tortured. Just as legal guilt requires punishment, unconscious psychological guilt requires punishment. Chronic dissatisfaction with life and psychological and physical symptoms are all ways of punishing ourselves for real or imagined misdeeds.

Forgiving ourselves implies a softening of the attitude, and accepting the ideas that we are good enough and that whatever we did in the past is over and done with. The only time we can change and correct our faulty attitudes is in the present. We are guiltless and blameless because we are part of God. The softening and letting go of self-condemnation allows us to be kinder and gentler towards ourselves and others. The more we experience God, the better people we become. If we like ourselves better, we like others better. This gives us less reason to come down on ourselves or others the next time.

Horney (1950) says that we all have an inner "idealized image" of ourselves. This is our version of how we should be: perfect. Then, whenever we fail at perfection we berate ourselves and punish ourselves. Horney urges us to let go of how we should be, forgive ourselves and accept how we really are. This opens up the possibility for us to get in touch with our "real self." The real self is composed of all our inner attributes, talents and potentialities. Our real self is a Spiritual self. It connects us to the divinity within. God does not want us to do what others have convinced us we should. God doesn't demand perfection. God wants us to develop our true selves in an accepting and forgiving manner.

Piero Ferrucci, in his delightful book, *What We May Be*, urges us to turn inward in forgiveness. The many psychosynthesis exercises in the book show us how to use our imaginative faculty to heal all levels of the psyche. Forgiveness is an attitude that enables us to approach these healing exercises. We must decide to let go of self-hate and approach our own divinity through the healing faculty of mind. The prayers and exercises enable us to come to terms with our emotional pain and inner conflicts as a prelude to finding our divinity.

Assagioli, the founder of psychosynthesis, was aware of his Godly side. When he was fourteen, he had what he calls a cosmic consciousness experience. A "voice" told him, "You will always be present to yourself." He vowed then to devote his life to understanding this experience, and to share it with others. Thus, he was the first to develop a psychological system that addressed both the personal unconscious and the superconscious. He saw that a gradual clearing away of a person's past traumas could reopen our connections to God. For Assagioli, God resided in the superconscious and could provide the power to heal the wounded self. The nature of God will shine through us when we work on all levels to become whole and holy.

A Hypnotic Trance to Develop Forgiveness

Just sit back and do whatever you need to do to become comfortable. You might want to move a bit...tense and relax each muscle group or just follow your breathing....Take whatever time you need to develop a deep sense of comfort...slowly let the warm relaxed feeling envelop your body and mind...feel your breath cleansing each and every cell in your lungs, heart, liver, kidneys, pancreas....cleansing every cell in every organ...you might want to picture a healing light, flowing around your body, relaxing your body and mind......all your nerves are calming down now...enabling you to slow down....as you slow down, you are aware of thoughts flowing through you...but you are much more than just thoughts, much more than just the feelings you observe, what kinds of feelings are flowing through you ? Is there any fear? anger? guilt? Can you connect these feelings to any events or people in your life? Let your mind follow the images, sensations, remembrances that lead you through your feelings into an event that seems to be the start of it all....Who is there? What is happening? How do you feel about it? Have you held onto those feelings? Would you like to let go of those feelings and move ahead with your life? Are you ready to forgive those others that may have hurt you? Would you like to ask the Higher Self or holy spirit to help you forgive? Can you feel the Higher Self as a source of love, faith and strength? Can you picture the holy spirit help-ing to turn you toward forgiveness? Can you see yourself forgiving someone? Would you like to experience the oneness of all creation by merging with the Higher Self? When you experience oneness, cosmic consciousness, you are naturally willing to forgive, are you not? Allow the oneness experience to give you the insight and strength to develop a new, more forgiving attitude toward others and toward yourself....Would you like to go still deeper into your soul...would you like to heal the guilt that was created when you thought you were sep-arated from God....recognize that this separation was your own illu-sion...created to protect you from fear...Do you realize that you no longer have to protect yourself? You were never really cut off from God...All is one...You live in a safe universe...So you can forgive your-self...You just made a mistake...You can correct this mistake now...by recognizing the power of forgiving yourself and others...All is one...So much peace and forgiveness grows out of that thought....remember to thank God for all the help in leading you to forgiveness, the true for-giveness you are choosing now with your new understanding...nobody meant to hurt you...they were afraid too...now you know...now you can forgive...now you can choose peace....feel it...experience it...and when your insight is sufficient to begin the forgiveness process your eyes will open and you will come back to the room, feeling good.

CHAPTER EIGHT

LOVE IS THE ANSWER: WHAT WAS THE QUESTION AGAIN?

I was riding in the car with my daughter who was eight years old at the time. Suddenly, she turned and asked me, "Hey dad, what's life *for* anyway?" I was not prepared to answer the question for her yet. But, there it was. I stammered, "I guess it's to love…as many people as you can…as much as you can." To this day, I can't improve on that answer. All I can do is try to clarify it, live it, and help others with it.

If life can be boiled down to one such simple word, why isn't the world a more loving place? Why don't we just get on with it and love each other? What is love anyway? Why do pronouncements of love sometimes seem like cliches? And why do we have such a hard time telling each other of our feelings of love?

According to the *Funk and Wagnall's Dictionary*, love is defined as, "a strong complex feeling or emotion causing one to appreciate, delight in and crave the presence or possession of another and to please or promote the welfare of the other; devoted affection or attachment." Notice that this definition seems to assume this love is for another separate person whom we want to please. It does not deal with love of God or even love of self. It certainly does not deal with love as an all encompassing principle of the universe. The idea of the essential unity and Oneness of Being is not included in Funk and Wagnall's definition of love. They define love strictly as a strong feeling between two persons. I imagine that linguists also think that universal love isn't important in our culture.

It appears that we reserve the term "love" for people that we like a lot for some reason-probably because they praise us and give us the things we want, or infatuate us romantically. People who frustrate us, don't give us what we want, or hurt our feelings we probably dislike or even hate. Since life gives us at least as many people who frustrate as gratify us we begin to see why the world isn't a more caring place.

As youngsters we usually divide people up into those we love and those we hate. Of course, life is not that simple. Our parents vary in their attitudes toward us, sometimes they give us what we want and sometimes they frustrate us. What do we do then? Usually, we repress the hated aspect and focus on the gratification of our parents. We try to see them as all good until we are mature enough to realize that everyone has a combination of gratifying and frustrating aspects.

In some cases, the opposite is true. We are mistreated and belittled so often we come to feel unlovable and blame our parents. If we can't decide, we alternate: loving them when we get what we want and hating them when they frustrate us. This trait (called "splitting" by psychologists) greatly confuses people, who generally call the resulting behavior "schizo". In actuality, there is nothing crazy about the behavior. People who "split" love you when you give them what they want, and hate you when you don't. If that sounds immature or narcissistic, it is. Yet, many of us behave that way at least some of the time. The more mature we are, the more we realize and accept that others are really a mixed bag.

Our immaturities stem from the hurts of our childhood, and as I've explained, our consequent rejection of God. Despite the fact that most parents (though not all) have good intentions, they have poor parenting skills and little knowledge of childhood development. Fear and guilt are often utilized to control difficult toddlers. Parents' own problems are often denied and projected or blamed on the innocent children.

Most of this is done unconsciously by parents who *think* they are act-ing in the best interests of the child. *In reality, children need uncondi-tional love, reasonable limits, tolerance, patience, genuineness and guidance appropriate to their age level.*

Such mature attitudes do not occur frequently enough, so instead of gradually developing in the fertile soil of loving limits, children are traumatized and stop growing emotionally at early ages. These are called "developmental arrests." When we are in developmental arrest, we unconsciously say to ourselves that we will not mature any further unless our caretakers (and significant others) treat us better. Immature people usually consciously *try* to love others, but the love is very conditional.

Because of this, most of us are accepted only conditionally by our parents and significant others. We get their approval only if we act cer-tain ways, do certain things and avoid behaviors and feelings they don't like. If we manage to streamline ourselves the way they want us to be, we may get enough approval to grow up reasonably well. However, the price we pay is high. We develop a "false self", with a large "shadow." In order to keep our feelings unconscious, we deny them and every-thing else in the unconscious, including God. In other words, we repress what we think we must (because significant others don't like it) and this becomes our unconscious shadow. Whatever we don't like in ourselves we will deny and project onto others whom we then dislike.

We cannot experience unconditional love if we have repressed God along with certain feelings. Remember, God can only be found in the "higher" part of the unconscious, *after* we have dealt with and accept-ed the nasty feelings we don't want to deal with that are in the "lower" or personal unconscious. When we realize this connection between repressed feelings and awareness of God, we also see that we can choose to reintegrate with God only after accepting our repressed feel-ings. Carl Jung felt that *wholeness* as a human being (which opens us up to Godliness) could only be achieved after the shadow feelings and behaviors were integrated into our conscious personalities. Before finding God, we must accept the parts of ourselves we don't like, even our potential to be nasty and mean.

The human propensity to blame others for their character traits which remind us of our shadow is one of the main stumbling blocks to loving each other more. Such "shadow" people are not gratifying to us. In fact we see them as dangerous in that they threaten to expose the hated portions of ourselves. Most people are just not mature enough to love others who are not gratifying, let alone those who remind us of what we have disowned in ourselves. It is easier to be judgmental and dislike these dangerous others.

In addition to "shadow figures", we have the so-called evil people to blame for many of the world's problems. The more clearly evil others are: e.g. murderers, the easier it is to judge them and desire their punishment. The vast majority of people I know do not favor rehabilitation for convicted criminals. They cannot see that anyone could become an evil murderer if pushed far enough. Thus, the choice of how most of us view murderers is simple: "You are evil and I am not, so you must be punished." They reject all arguments about the childhood abuse that causes criminality and the Spiritual, loving attitude needed to help such people.

Although I recognize that rehabilitating criminals is a difficult project, it does happen. Witness the furor over the Paul Simon Broadway show, "*The Capeman*." Many people picketed the show, claiming Simon was glorifying the murderer, Salvador Agron. They completely ignored that Agron had rehabilitated himself and, refused to consider what he went through in his early years that caused his criminal behavior. To express compassion or invite penitence (rethinking), is thought to be too softhearted. As a friend said to me recently, "Sam, you are mush!" How hard hearted we have become to favor revenge over compassion!

The compassionate attitude *does not* blame the victim. Nor does it say that it is all right to harm others. It is *not acceptable* to harm others. However, once harm occurs, we must look at the true causes of such unnatural actions and work with them in a compassionate way to prevent such actions in the future. This applies to the criminal as well as to potential future criminals. Where such rehabilitation has not worked, of course, prisoners need to remain locked up until they are transformed. In many cases, such transformation will never occur. And yes, I believe we as a society must pay for their upkeep. As a society we cause the problem by raising so many children so badly. I agree with Alice Miller. All criminals are abused or neglected children.

So What Do I Do If I Wasn't Loved

There are many things you can do if you feel you weren't loved. The first thing to do is recognize that you can't go back and get that kind of unconditional love retroactively. You needed it then. You must *face that fact and grieve that loss*. Then you can go to the next step, self acceptance, shadow and all. It is important to realize that this grief may take a long time and, when it is allowed to surface, will let out many powerful emotions. What you will begin to see, however, is that you are really all right, just the way you are, even with all your "forbidden" emotions: shame, anger, guilt, hate etc. In fact, you will see that a lot of your present hate is simply displaced retaliation for harsh treatment you endured in the past. Grieving initiates a softening process which eventually results in reconnecting to Spirit, and in you loving a lot more people.

Is there any Way to Skip the Grieving Process?

There is no way to skip the grieving process. Many people try to do this by becoming "Spiritual", or "Holy" before they are ready. The inevitable result is a short circuiting of the true psycho-spiritual healing they really need. Psycho-spiritual healing involves working toward letting go of your identification purely with your self-interest. Instead, you begin to identify more with the greater good, out of experiential knowledge that we are really all one at the deepest level. *But,* and this is a big *but,* it takes strength to ally yourself with the "Higher Self." The grieving process strengthens you (by incorporating the shadow) in preparation for allying the ego with the Higher Self. The ego never wants to do this and can be very tricky. The Twelve-step programs urge us to "let go, let God." This is a great idea but it can only be done after we have incorporated our shadow, and have taken responsibility for our negative emotions and attitudes.

There is one way, however, of speeding up the grieving process, and that is in turning to the Higher Power in prayer. I believe the Higher Power supplies the strength to do two vital things: First, it can help us face our own negativity and shadow. Second, God can give us the strength to endure what has been called the "dark night of the soul." This is a time when everything seems, dark, dreary and hopeless. Contrary to what some people believe, our life does not become immediately wonderful as soon as we decide to pray and become spiritual. The Higher Power is a loving energy source that seems to help us develop the feeling of wholeness that we need while we go through the healing process. This process will always include some pain, and sometimes it will include a lot of pain and suffering. But joining with the Higher Power through prayer does give us strength. This support was most clearly evident in one of the most interesting cases I have had so far, the treatment of Sandy.

Your Soul Can Heal You

Sandy was a beautiful child who suffered much abuse in her enmeshed domineering family. The basic rule of the family was, "The oldest child must stay here and be miserable with us, she cannot leave and become independent and happy." After much physical and mental abuse, Sandy followed the rule. Outwardly, she was very successful in young adulthood. She became a fashion model and went to Paris, making large amounts of money and giving all of it away. Ultimately, her low self-esteem caused her to crash into a "nervous breakdown." She returned home and spent three years languishing in her parents' attic, unable to do anything. Out of total desperation, she was led to pray. This was the start of her movement toward healing and wholeness.

As she describes it: "After three years of hanging on without change or hope of change, I just let go. I gave up my life. I gave up my ideas and dreams as I had known them. I stopped clinging. Without even realizing it I let go. I let go of my life. Then something happened…deep from the bottom of my being arose a different feeling…there must be someone, somewhere, who can help people who are as afraid as I am…This, I realized months later, was prayer." (Hubert, Unpublished Manuscript,)

Sandy discovered that while her ego self had given up, her soul had not. She was too wounded, split, and fractured to go on without prayer and help from the soul level. Sandy began therapy soon after that and gradually improved. She began to realize she was a gifted spiritual teacher. Her particular gift was what she termed "soul reading." She is able to learn a great deal about a person's potential, gifts and problem issues merely by being in their presence. After several years of hiding her talent, she began to do these soul readings and she even wrote a book about it. But she felt she could not publish the book and become more widely known. This would be a violation of what she called "the contract" with her parents. The contract stipulated that she was not allowed to be independent, successful or happy. She still suffered from low self-esteem, rigidity, instability and unhappiness. The key *seemed* to be to release the contract. But, no amount of therapy seemed to budge this understanding with her parents.

She began to think that perhaps she had some past life karma to clear up before she could be independent and happy. It was at this point that she was referred to me for past life regression.

Now, this form of therapy, similar to age regression-through hypnosis has proved successful with many of my clients, even clients who didn't believe in past lives. Thus, I was willing to attempt it with her. She proved to be a good hypnotic subject and did experience several past lives while under hypnosis. Yet, things were not changing much. There was still that contract.

It was at this point that the regressions began to change. Her "inner child," little Sandy, began to speak, stomping around angrily because she was being ignored by adult Sandy. Suddenly, her soul addressed little Sandy and adult Sandy with the most basic, healing message of all, *"You are love, and you are light.*

She phrased this basic message a little differently to each part of herself, but the idea stressed the essential oneness of her being. The hypnotic trances were transformed into prayerful meditations, wherein she affirmed her identity as love and light to each level of her being. "Little Sandy" was delighted with the attention and stopped sabotaging adult Sandy's efforts toward independence and happiness. Adult Sandy was also thrilled to see how knowledge of the truth of oneness helped her maintain happiness and stability. She began doing these prayerful meditations daily, writing down the messages she needed to hear each day. The messages kept reminding her that she "is love and light." I noticed that she began to literally glow during these meditations. The spiritual energy became intense and her life is healing rapidly.

As a psychologist, my experiences with Sandy made me re-think everything I thought about spirituality and healing. I now believe that there are two different levels, the psychological and the spiritual, which are connected. Psychological work is a laborious process because the law of cause and effect is operating. The traumas, negative beliefs, fearful imagery etc. cause depression, anxiety, physical problems etc. Working through these traumas by prayer and therapy helps strengthen us enough for the Spiritual level to be touched. At the Spiritual level, there is no law of cause and effect. Thus, instantaneous physical healings *sometimes* occur. The reason these amazing healings do not happen more often is that most of us are firmly entrenched in the physical and psychological idea of separateness. Thus, we must go through the law of cause and effect. If we somehow leap to the Spiritual level, amazing things like instantaneous healings may take place. Of course, as mystic teacher Joel Goldsmith reminds us, if we have reached the Spiritual level, we already *know* that all is one, and we are all right whether our bodies are healed or not. I believe these healings, whether slow or instant, psychological or mystical, are related to readiness to surrender and accept Spiritual matters as more important than material matters. The more we ally ourselves with Spirit, the more likely we are to heal. But more on that in the next chapter. The case of Sandy is interesting because she is healing so well without much cognitive analysis of her traumatic past. Instead, we meditate together and allow the healing to occur, with constant reminders of the truth that she is love and light.

This is *true* self-love (not narcissism) that is healing Sandy. Her hard work in therapy seems to have made her strong enough to accept the truth that she *is* love and light at each level of her being. She can now, with this knowledge, publish her excellent book, *Your Soul Can Heal You,* and help others. She is not violating any contract with her parents because there *is no contract.* We are all love and light and the implications of this are enormous. Spiritual truth can heal the psyche and even the body, sometimes in miraculous fashion, *if we are ready.* This book is about getting ready through prayer.

CHAPTER NINE

LISTENING TO THE STILL, SMALL VOICE

Surrender is usually viewed in a negative sense. When I bring up the concept in therapy I usually get the attitude, "why should I surrender??! Notice the underlined "I". It sounds like an ego problem again. It is. Again, I am defining ego here as that conscious executive function we all have. It is the part of us that has awareness most of the time, makes judgements, decisions, remembers previous events and learnings and applies them. It is what we normally think of as our "self." In reality, it is only a small part of our Self, and who we really are in toto.

Back to Washburn

In earlier sections I have alluded to several theorists including Ken Wilber, Carl Jung, Roberto Assagioli and Michael Washburn. In this chapter, I want to emphasize Washburn because he explains ego development, as well as the importance of voluntarily surrendering to God (which he terms the Ground of Being) later in life. He sees the ego as a necessary part of development which eventually must be transcended.

Washburn discusses three phases of normal development: pre-egoic, egoic and trans-egoic. The pre-egoic stage consists roughly of the first two years of life. During this period, the ego develops gradually through interaction with primary care givers and other people in the environment. First, at birth, there is only a Ground of Being (God), individualizing through the baby's experiences in the world. During this stage, God dominates the fledgling ego. The ego is formed out of experience. Initially, it is mostly a "body ego," completely tied to bodily comfort and pleasure. If a "good enough" caregiver keeps it fairly comfortable, it slowly develops a sense of healthy separateness from other people. This is a natural development and has nothing to do with the Spiritual ideal of realizing that beneath our separateness is really oneness. An unavoidable side effect of this normal separation-individuation process is psychological discomfort.

In a good environment, with good enough care, the baby moves from the bliss of oneness with mother to the pain of separation and individuation. The emerging toddler slowly begins to realize that the world (unlike the pre-birth umbilical cord) doesn't automatically give what she needs. There is inevitably a fearful, angry interplay when the caregiver doesn't give what the baby needs on demand. As the baby becomes more autonomous (crawling, walking, talking) more ambivalence and conflict is generated. The angry, fearful, guilty feelings on both the child's and parent's part are usually seen by the child as dangerous and must be repressed to maintain stability. In order to gain more autonomy and freedom, the toddler must repress not only dangerous feelings, but some of the dependency needs. She needs the mother too much to fully realize such fearful and angry feelings.

In repressing dependency needs and negative feelings, the toddler must also repress the Godly part of the unconscious. Just as other people are now seen as separate and apart from her, so is God separate and apart from her. Time marches on. We all make many emotional adjustments. There are a number of physical, psychological and spiritual lessons to be learned and many painful emotions must be repressed. At various stages the world looks different, until, at a certain point, perhaps early adolescence, this "original repression" is completed. At this point, the separate ego is developed enough to take charge. It's first strategy is to move the base of operations up from the body to the head.

The adolescent and young adult now feel ready to take on what appears to be the (separate, outside) world.

The Egoic Stage

The ego now thinks it is in complete charge of her life, and feels a pull to develop a separate, secure, successful identity. It thinks it is in charge of creating security out of separateness (God has usually been repressed completely by this time or is seen as an outside power which must be dealt with). Many people spend a lifetime at the task of trying to create security through a strong ego. They revere the idea that they are simply a body with an ego in charge that must deal with the unpredictable world and in some cases God's desires. Some of us think we are succeeding and that the world of separateness and chaos is all there is (the rich, the famous, the successful etc.). Others do not do as well in the world and continue to struggle, believing the world and its problems is all that is. They often think of themselves as underachievers or losers. As we mentioned in Chapter Three, both of these groups are stuck at the egoic stage. During this stage the ego dominates the Ground of Being.

However, there are many people who start to feel (usually in mid-life) that there must be something more to life than just a meaningless struggle with the world. Sometimes, there is just a nagging feeling, but more often there are traumatic life experiences that almost insist that the Spiritual search begin. This is a call to initiate the *trans-egoic* (beyond the ego) search for meaning.

Washburn recommends that meditation be initiated to foster this search. He warns that it is not an easy process but that the rewards are great—a more integrated, loving, secure, Selfhood. A secure Self grows out of a knowledge that the divine Ground of Being is and always will be, dominant over the ego. The ego, in recognizing this fact can now gain strength, *by allying with the Higher Self*, to deal with the inevitable problems of life and deal with them better. Also, the times of joy, happiness and bliss are more intense. The trip, Washburn tells us, is worth the pain.

So what are we surrendering? We are surrendering the false sense that our ego is all we have to cope with the world. In biblical terms we are bowing to the king. But this is not an outside physical king. It is the king inside our consciousness, the source of all Being, the fountainhead of oneness, God. In order to do this we must consciously say to our ego, "I know there is more to me than just you. You have done what you thought you had to, but now I realize that there is much more to my Being, a much more powerful part of me must be put in charge. From now on, God will be in charge of the life process. We will accept our Spiritual "lesson plan" gratefully and learn of the unending love that lies beyond the illusion of separateness that we used to worship. We are no longer going to waste our time and energy being concerned with security operations against others. We are going to expend our energy to see the inner light of truth, and that truth will set us free. Security grows out of the idea of oneness, not out of fortifying ourselves against "enemies." All is one and that is all we need to see. We need to surrender and ally ourselves with the Higher Self to see it. Goodbye negative beliefs. Goodbye to fears of lack, harm, humiliation, abandonment, death. Hello to source of All that Is: peace, harmony, abundance, fulfillment. I surrender my limited and negative beliefs and I replace them with Godly beliefs. I surrender to the immanent and transcendent source of all Being. I surrender to God. I hereby direct my energy to do its best to follow God's will. I join with the Higher Self, knowing, eventually that God's will and my own will, will merge and become one.

Allying with God's Will

The first step in allying with God's will is *intention*. In other words we must want it and want it badly. It is amazing how often I hear patients repeat the phrase, "we'll see what happens" in reference to any problem in their lives. Though it is true we don't totally control what happens, we do have input. What we aim for has *a lot to do with what happens*. I usually reply, "What do you want to happen?" This is followed by a pause. Sometimes, just that question clarifies the goal. The person is then able to say what they want to have happen. Other times, they reply that they really don't know what they want. In both cases, the problem is usually that they are afraid to declare and state what they want for fear they won't be able to get it.

This preliminary interchange usually leads to a discussion of the Buddhist concept of non-attachment. That is, you must become comfortable with pursuing a goal and not getting the result you *think* you want. According to my understanding of Buddhism, it is fine to *want* something as long as you don't *absolutely have to have it*. In other words, we can and should be involved in the process of life *and* all results are good. The suffering comes from the clinging to one particular result. If any outcome is good, you are free to put as much intention and energy as you want into the project or goal. Then, you can watch with great interest and absorption as the fruits of your effort are sown.

If all of the above is true, it would be of great benefit to declare that you *want to do God's will*. For those who prefer a universal concept, you can declare, *I want to manifest my destiny according to the will of my Higher Self.* Either way, you are placing an order, with great intention, to the most powerful energy source there is. You then declare yourself open to all signs as to how to proceed with actions, without any attachment to any particular result. It is the action, the process that matters, not the result.

In turning your will and intention over to your Higher Self or God, you must be willing to *drop* more selfish, ego goals. For example, you may or may not get more money or stuff as a result of your efforts. *But*, you will surely find your days more meaningful, productive and happy as you do things for the greater good *as well as* for your own good. As you turn your will over to God, eventually, your will coincides with God's will. You must have faith that in turning things over to God, your own needs and those of your family will be taken care of.

Turning things over to God means letting go of immaturity, narcissism, strictly materialistic goals, selfishness and all the rest of the things that seem to promise happiness but ultimately end up with disappointment. To use an extreme example, I don't think Mother Teresa was disappointed with her life, whereas, Marilyn Monroe was. Marilyn's lack of love in childhood condemned her to seek love and meaning through fame and fortune. This perilous road never works.

Some people think that turning things over to God's will is a cop out, an avoidance of personal responsibility. Nothing could be further from the truth. Turning a problem over to God's will indicates that you are ready to do your part in the plan, as soon as you realize what it is. You take full responsibility for your choices and behaviors. You are simply getting guidance and power from a source that is by nature, loving and unselfish. Theologian Emmet Fox suggests that when you find yourself puzzled by a problem, "stressed out", or unable to "figure out" what to do, just meditate on the word "God." The answer will come, but *YOU have to act, and take responsibility for your choices.* Chapter Ten will examine this concept of responsibility and action in depth. But first we need practice on turning our will over to the highest part of ourselves.

A Hypnotic Exercise to Turn Your Will Over to God

Suppose you have made a decision, out of desperation, frustration or aggravation, and you want to turn your will over to God. You have the intention but you don't know how to start. Here is a hypnotic exercise to get you started. It utilizes both post-hypnotic suggestion and prayer to lessen identification with the body and ego, while directing the will toward Godly, transpersonal pursuits. It is an attempt to promote "mystical" consciousness.

Research in hypnosis by Dr. Paul Sacerdote has indicated that a mystical state of consciousness is useful in many ways—including pain control. Sacerdote's work validated the earlier work of author and spiritual healer Frederick Bailes. At the turn of the last century, Bailes was diagnosed with diabetes. This was before the invention of synthetic insulin, so he was told he would soon die. Since he felt he was not ready to die yet, he developed a technique for identifying with the infinite. He was healed, and lived a long life as a metaphysical writer and lecturer. Bailes' technique for developing a mystical state of consciousness will be integrated into the exercise. Once again, read it into a tape recorder in a slow, melodious, gentle voice. You may listen as often as you wish—but never while operating a motor vehicle.

Now, just be aware of your breathing...With each breath your body is becoming more relaxed...whenever it would be more comfortable, your eyes will close, and you will be able to drift into a very comfortable state of consciousness...you don't have to do anything...as these words reach your mind, your body enjoys progressive relaxation in every muscle and cell. You are now surrounded by a soothing atmosphere of absolute calmness and serenity...you are totally safe and protected...surrounded, safely in every direction by wider and wider concentric circles of luminous serenity, absolute calmness...you are able to safely bathe and comfortably breathe in the center of these transparent spheres...while luminous calmness all around you penetrates even more deeply within your body and permeates your mind. Little by little you become free of all concerns, free of all fears, thoughts, feelings...(30 sec. pause)

I wonder if you would like to go on a pleasant trip now...you are able to lift your consciousness up now...temporarily leaving your body safely behind as you rise up into the air, higher and higher...above the trees...above all buildings...above the atmosphere...you can see the Earth now, peacefully floating in space...from a distance the earth seems so beautifully blue and green...the most peaceful feeling of all can come over your awareness now. You may develop now true insight and knowledge into the universe...it may be unexplainable in words but you are gaining much that you can explain in words when you rejoin your body...it may be a mystical feeling of oneness...or perhaps something entirely different, yet beneficial feeling...experience it in its fullness.

You now have the knowledge of how to attain a mystical state of mind...thus, you are attuning your will with God's will...you can use this experiential knowledge in practical ways to help others and yourself. You can safely go back now and rejoin your body and ego back on Earth...when you awaken you will feel different...somehow better...you will find yourself praying regularly...thanking God for the strength to progressively make the changes that are needed, in your attitude. You are noticing small differences and you attitude is becoming more positive and remaining more peaceful and loving than ever before...you are able to regularly turn your will over to God's will...your life is becoming better in so many ways. You will wait until you are fully awake and reoriented to your body before you drive a car, or cross a street...counting backwards from five...you will awaken at one, 4...3...2...1. Awakening feeling refreshed relaxed and alert.

As you can see, joining with the "Higher Self" is not complicated once you truly want to do it. But what a struggle it is for most people to *want* to do it. Most of us are afraid of losing lifelong habits that we cherish so much. Some people assume that surrendering will lead to some sort of monklike asceticism, or a loss of all drive to succeed. Although that is possible, it is not probable. Most likely the life you lead will not be significantly different from the lifestyle you had before surrendering. However, *your attitudes* will be significantly improved.

As *A Course in Miracles* suggests, you will be called to do such things as remove all "attack thoughts," to pray for guidance, view situations from a "win-win" perspective, to forgive others (not out of pity but out of equality), and "choose peace" instead of worrying or being upset. In short, you will likely be called to become a sort of ambassador of good will in a world full of fear, competition, hate and greed. Now, do you want to surrender to God's will? His will is for you to become a part of the solution instead of continuing the problem. That is why *A Course in Miracles* is called an attitudinal healing process.

Listening

An important part of joining with the Higher Self is learning to *listen* to what has traditionally been called, "the still, small voice." This voice is very different from a thought, and altogether different from a hallucinated, "schizophrenic" voice. Schizophrenic voices are always negative. They are inner fears and self-hate, projected outward into an external voice. The still small voice is positive, loving and helpful. It leads to more peace, not fear. It sometimes appears during prayers, and at other times when completely unbidden, as in the following case

Maria's Inner Voice

Maria, who was described in Chapter Five, states that she has always had an inner voice, helping her. When she was a child, the voice told her to be careful, her new house would shortly burn down. Sure enough, there was a fire and the house did burn down. The whole family was able to escape due to Maria's warning. Twenty-five years later, the voice told her of another fire. She forgot about it though, and six months later the warning was repeated, including even the specific location of the fire: on the second floor of a brick, two-family house she and her husband owned. The next day, the house burned down due to a short circuit in a plugged in toaster. She and her husband were out, shopping for groceries. No one was harmed. The voice has also given her correct information on business ventures and showed her an image of her daughter before she was born. The likelihood is that Maria has benevolent spirit guides helping her. There are, however, other types of inner voices that help.

Voices of Deceased Relatives

A woman, with no belief in spiritual voices or life after death told me the following story: She was sitting in a coffee shop, ordering coffee when the waiter asked if she wanted sugar. A "voice" interrupted and said, "She's so sweet, she doesn't need sugar." Startled, she wondered if it wasn't the voice of her recently deceased father. It sounded like his voice. The experience "different than just a thought," and that she had not even been thinking about her father.

A Gentle Therapist

My friend and colleague, Tully Ruderman passed away recently. Tully was a funny, wise and gentle woman who helped many people through the agony of a slow death from cancer. Ironically, she herself died of cancer. She had been very close with her husband, Rudy, who was naturally overcome with grief when she passed away. For months, Rudy walked around miserable. Everything seemed weary, stale, flat and unprofitable. Then, one day, he had what he termed an epiphanous moment. He was watching a bird, fly around his yard when he suddenly felt happy !! After a few seconds he remembered that his beloved wife was gone and he had no right to be happy. At this moment he heard Tully's voice say, "Schmuck !! Why are you letting your thoughts interfere with your natural happiness!! Apparently, Tully was still doing therapy from the "other side," helping the man she loved the most. Tully's therapy worked.

Rudy recognized that he could still be happy, even though Tully was physically gone. He had let his chattering conscious mind, laden with guilt destroy a natural, happy moment. Inner voices can help us, whether they are of deceased relatives, spirit guides or our own intuitive Higher Self.

Some Personal Experiences

One night, driving home from *A Course in Miracles* class, I heard an inner voice say, "Get to the right." I mentally argued with the voice, saying that I had to get to the left to go over the George Washington Bridge. "Get to the right !!!" the voice insisted. Reluctantly, I moved right whereupon I suddenly saw a terrible traffic jam due to an accident ahead on the left ramp. I was thus able to avoid the jam up and get home quickly, thanks to my inner voice. I believe that I was more open to my Higher Self because we had been talking about the voice of the Holy Spirit in class.

Another time the voice came to me while I was showering, "Go to Synagogue," it said. Again I argued, "but I have to care for my two year old daughter this morning; she won't let me pray." "Go to synagogue." So I went. My daughter was a doll, sitting quietly and letting me pray.

Still another time, my landlord, a behavioral psychologist, asked me to remove my Spiritual magazines from the waiting room, lest his patients think he was a nut. "It's time to move to your own place", said the voice. This time I didn't argue. I followed my inner guidance and gave him notice even though I had no new office yet. He told me I was crazy to give him notice but I did and quickly found a new place right down the block, where I was much more content.

What Are These Voices?

It seems like these voices could be a number of things. It could be a loving deceased relative. It could be our own Higher Self or a Spiritual guide, wanting to help. I have had and heard about enough experiences, however, to know that there are some benevolent forces with higher vision who will help when asked, but *we have to be willing to listen and act.*

When the voice proposes actions leading to feelings of peace and happiness and is for the good of all concerned, it is to be heeded. If it seems to be negative, greedy, competitive or selfish, it is probably the voice of the fearful ego, trying to motivate us to gain advantage over others. When this is the case, don't heed this ego voice. Instead, I go back and pray for more guidance for a direction that will lead to the greatest good of all concerned.

Listening to the Voice in Prayer

Most religious traditions emphasize a certain liturgy. That is, they want you to pray certain prayers at certain times. The emphasis, however, is on the repetition of the prayers, not waiting for any answers. The more esoteric branches of religions, however, advocate praying from the *heart* and listening for answers. The *still small voice* wants to help. The goal is more peace and love than before. Ultimately, enlightenment will ensue.

Psychologist Wayne Dyer defines enlightenment as peace. He feels that a truly enlightened person will always respond peacefully. *A Course In Miracles* tells us that at any time we may choose peace instead of an upsetting emotional reaction. My experience has been that choosing peace is a good habit which takes time to develop. I suggest you begin this development now.

There are many parallels to this process of attuning yourself to inner guidance in "third and fourth force" (humanistic or spiritual) psychotherapy. There is an interactive process that goes on within the unconscious that parallels the prayer process. Jung, for example, had his patients amplify their dreams later, through active imagination. Assagioli had scores of exercises to utilize the imaginative faculty of the Higher Self to heal the psyche. Milton Erickson used metaphor, confusion and indirect suggestion to still the conscious mind (ego) and prod the unconscious to creatively use its resources to heal perplexing life problems. George Groddek, a physician in Freud's time, was a pioneer in healing physical ailments through psychological means. He knew the unconscious was superior to the ego and stated, "We are lived by the it." (the unconscious) Though none of these theorists mentioned inner voices, God, or prayer per se, they were all accessing unconscious and superconscious levels of the mind to produce healing.

Too much of what passes for psychotherapy today accesses only the conscious mind. In order for the therapy to be truly successful, there must be some interaction with the unconscious, through prayer, meditation, hypnosis, imagery or dream work. Such methods honor the idea that each of us is more than just a body with a conscious mind (ego). Below the surface is the personal unconscious (which must be dealt with for Spiritual growth) and the superconscious-Godly realm which can provide guidance, power, and above all, love, to make the actual changes in our daily lives. Much of what therapists call "resistance" to change is the ego's stubborn refusal to surrender to the part of ourselves that is superior. Prayer can help us resolve our resistance toward beneficial changes. Sooner or later, we must surrender and join with the superconscious.

Surrender is used here only in the positive sense. We are surrendering to the highest, purest level of ourselves, the level that ultimately will take precedence anyway. For as Groddek said, we are really being "lived" by the unconscious. God enters our lives through the unconscious and the people and events of our lives. In order to produce harmony and peace we should *accept* the circumstances, lives, events and people who show up unexpectedly. As long as we are alive, there are Spiritual lessons to be learned, and Spiritual knowledge to be remembered. This is the true meaning of surrender. Surrender is allying ourselves with our Higher Self. Our prayers should be directed toward this type of surrender to the part of us that wants peace and is willing to let go of negativity, selfishness and fear. Now we are ready to move on to an examination of personal responsibility within the surrender to the Higher Self.

CHAPTER TEN

GOOD NEWS: GOD HELPS THOSE WHO HELP THEMSELVES

The focus of this chapter is responsibility-personal responsibility. In order for our lives to improve we must take maximum responsibility. This may seem paradoxical to the message of the last chapter—surrender—but it is not. We must remember that we are *co-creators* of our lives. God provides the energy, circumstances, strength, love and general lesson plans (enlightenment) for our lives. We provide the personal belief system (reflected in events and feelings about events), will, decisions and action on those decisions. It is a mistake to think that all we have to do is pray and God will handle the rest for us. After we pray, we must use God's strength, guidance and inspiration to make the best decisions we can about our lives and *take action*. We have free will, but we must also be willing to accept the results of our decisions. Most importantly, we must realize that we control our reactions to events via our attitudes. The real healing involves choosing kind, peaceful and loving attitudes, no matter what gets thrown at us.

There is a Jewish *midrash* (teaching story) about creation that demonstrates this truth. It seems that God was getting a little bored with the angelic realms. Angels always followed God's will, since they had to by their nature. So God created the animals, but they didn't have any free will either. They were just programmed by instinct to survive. Finally, God created human beings. He gave us free will in the hope that even though we could choose to go against him, we would make the free choice to follow his ways. Obviously, most of us have not made this choice, so we must accept responsibility for the choices we have made.

The Existentialists

The existentialists were an interesting and varied group of philosophers and (more recently) psychotherapists dedicated to the idea of personal responsibility. Some of the most influential thinkers in this area have been Friedreich Nietzsche, Jean Paul Sartre, and Soren Kierkegaard (philosophers), Paul Tillich (theologian), Ludwig Binswanger, Victor Frankl and Irwin Yalom (psychotherapists). Each of these eminent men have provided insights into the importance of responsibility in developing a meaningful life.

Nietzsche is best known for his concept of the "will to power." He felt that our fundamental drive was to live up to our potential. In order to do this, we have to make choices and take responsibility for ourselves. This requires courage, which opens up the way to authentic Being. Thus, we are urged to stop drifting about aimlessly and to see that we *are our choices.* The so-called "superman" was seen as a person willing to make choices and follow through with action. Unfortunately, Nietzsche also believed that God, the creator, was dead. I believe that he was talking about God as an external force, not the God within. Thus, he confused ego with our Higher Self and fell prey to a belief that his ego was a godlike superman. Jung called this ego inflation. Nevertheless, Nietzsche did properly stress responsibility.

Jean Paul Sartre, in his book, *Nausea*, wrote that individuals are "doomed to freedom," and are responsible for their acts as well as failures to act. He wanted to liberate us from "bad faith" and get us to take responsibility for ourselves. He felt that our moment of illumination would come when we take responsibility for our actions. The reason why he felt we were doomed is that ultimately he saw no Higher Power to help out. In his philosophy, meaning had to be created *by ourselves*, through our decisions. He had the right idea about responsibility, but he couldn't sense the help available from spirit.

Soren Kierkegaard was a Danish philosopher and practicing Christian. He sought truth by questioning the dominant rationalist philosophy of the nineteenth century. He saw the central problem of humankind as: "I exist now, I am aware of it, now what do I do?" Kierkegaard was seeking ways of becoming an authentic individual. In order to be authentic, he felt we had to take responsibility for our lives. By placing responsibility at the center of his philosophy, Kierkegaard is usually considered the father of existentialist philosophy.

Ludwig Binswanger was a psychiatrist who felt that "mental illness" was not a disease, but a disruption of the human condition. Symptoms were seen as an avoidance of the responsibility for oneself. He felt that by courageously facing one's existentially based issues, life would become enriched. The job of the therapist was to *understand* the patient. Out of this understanding the patient would experience herself as unique, and gain the courage to be real in the present. Binswanger felt that the patient needed an experience, not an explanation. He felt that taking responsibility for immediate experience was the key to healing. Again though, he left out the Spiritual element.

Irwin Yalom is a contemporary psychotherapist, specializing in the existential approach to psychotherapy. In his book, *Existential Psychotherapy*, he notes that the four basic existential issues which must be faced are; death, freedom, meaning and responsibility. He feels that symptoms such as anxiety and depression are caused by looking into the future and seeing the need to take responsibility for upcoming events. In other words, symptoms are a replacement for taking responsibility for an uncertain future. The person feels too weak to face death or to create meaning through using her freedom to make good choices.

Instead, symptoms are formulated so that responsibility can be avoid-ed. This is done unconsciously, nevertheless, it is done. Again, Yalom stresses the importance of responsibility without turning to spirit for help and guidance.

Paul Tillich was a Lutheran Theologian in the early twentieth centu-ry. In his book, *The Courage to Be*, he encouraged his readers to accept the notion that there are certain inevitable anxieties that are inherent in the human condition, including a fear of non-being. He believed there-fore in the importance of responsibility and action. He stated that, "the self affirmation of a being is the stronger the more non-being it can take into itself." For Tillich, as a believer in God, this was an opening to gain courage by opening to the transcendent. He was saying it is normal to be afraid but if you open up to that which is beyond your own ego, you will gain strength. You must, however, *take action* in this direction to fulfill your destiny.

Victor Frankl spent his entire life creating a psychology of mean-ing and responsibility. Frankl, a survivor of a concentration camp felt that it was absolutely necessary to make difficult choices to create meaning in one's life. He made the choice to preserve his book, *Man's Search For Meaning*, on scraps of paper while he was in the death camp. Thus, he took responsibility for his and the book's meaningful survival and this helped him survive. He stressed the importance of choosing a positive attitude at all times, pointing out that no matter how bad things may seem, you always have control over your attitude. The ultimate responsibility for your life is your own through free will and free choice.

Note that Tillich and Frankl put a Spiritual spin on what had start-ed out as an atheistic philosophy. They both believed in God and the power of faith. Yet, they both believed we need the courage to take responsibility and act, no matter how badly our life might be going. Frankl was particularly adamant about his hatred of suicide. He felt that Spiritually, there was always some reason to live, and it was the individual's responsibility to find it. These spiritual existentialists were both theists. That is, they had faith that there is a creative intelligence in an ordered universe. Nevertheless, the individual has to take responsibility and courageously make choices.

Gurdjieff

Russian mystic George Gurdjieff had a saying which is most appropriate here: "Pray like there was no need to take action, but take action like there was no such thing as prayer." As a mystic, Gurdjieff knew that at bottom, all is one. Yet, he also knew that we must continue to live in a world of seeming multiplicity and separation. Thus, he urged his followers to focus their intentions, no matter what they did. If they were praying, pray from the heart. However, they must also take *responsibility* to act. So he urged his followers to take action as if there is no such thing as prayer. He told us not to wait for God to do miraculous things, which he saw as magic. The miracle is our loving intent in taking action to help ourselves, as well as others, the world etc. We must recognize our miraculous ability to act in a responsible, loving fashion.

A Course in Miracles

A Course in Miracles encourages us to pray for guidance, then take action based on this guidance. The action may be a physical act, or it may be the most important action of all, which is *changing our view of things*. There is always a way of looking at things differently to create a "win-win" situation. As soon as we "choose peace" rather than create conflict, we become open to viewing the situation in another way. The peace is in not resisting what is beyond our control. Instead, we go with the event and learn from it. "All things are lessons God would have us learn." This is part of taking responsibility for our lives. Instead of insisting it go our way and pouting if it doesn't, we ask the Higher Power for help in seeing things differently. This changes everything and opens the way for the miracle of love and compassion for ourselves and those who used to be so frustrating to us.

How to Control Your Anger

Controlling our anger is not repressing it or stuffing it. Rather, we transcend it. I believe in an effective three step program developed by psychologist Alvin Marks of Alpine, California. Dr. Marks agrees with the research of Carol Tavris which reversed the old idea that it was good to get your anger out. Both Tavris and Marks find that expressing a lot of anger just leads to more anger. However, controlling and transcending anger as it appears is helpful. Here is Dr. Marks' easily understandable and usable technique.

Whenever we feel irritated, frustrated or angry, we must redefine it as helplessness. We say to ourselves, "things are not going my way, I have no control over them, so I am feeling irritated. I am therefore helpless to control this person or situation." This sets the stage for the *responsible actions necessary*.

First, we must *surrender* to the fact that this event has occurred. We cannot undo the event. We may react and take actions now in light of what happened, but the upsetting event happened. We must accept this and surrender the control we really never had anyway.

Second, we must *pinpoint* the particular aspect of the other person's behavior that made us feel irritated. This will lead us to what Jung called our "shadow." What this means is that we are probably angry because the other person did something that we might have wanted to do, but didn't. We have it under control, but they don't. Even worse, they seem to be getting away with it. We rationalize that we would never do that and even if we did we'd never get away with it. Jung correctly perceived that we all have a shadow and are all capable of doing pretty bad things if pushed hard enough. We don't like to admit this but it's true. This realization leads to the final step, which is forgiveness.

We *forgive* the behavior not from a position of superiority, but from the insight that the alleged insult was nothing personal. The other person did it because it is the only way they know how to survive psychologically. They would have done it to anyone to survive. Each of us is also capable of annoying behavior in order to psychologically survive. Thus, letting it go allows us to move on without holding on to hidden anger and resentment. It is for our good as well as the good of others. This is the underlying truth in the *Course in Miracles,* win-win, way of looking at things. The *Course* tells us not to compound the error by making it real. Forgiving involves letting it go—overlooking it. It is much more important to face our own shadow than to blame others-who are in fact our brothers. Facing our own shadow is a difficult but marvelously rewarding process. It stops us from projecting our problems onto others and brings us peace of mind and spirit.

Prayer can help us to take this *responsibility*. It aids us first, by giving us strength and impetus. And second, by helping us see beyond the limited egoic point of view. Once we *experience* mystical oneness through prayer and meditation, we can drop the haughty, superior, judgmental stance and accept life as it is, wonderful and mysterious. We are all here to teach each other valuable lessons in living and loving. I like to recall what Joni Mitchell wrote: "I've looked at life from both sides now, both win and lose and still somehow, it's life's illusions I recall, I really don't know life at all." In order to really know life, we must see the illusions of the ego and turn to the higher way of looking at things.

The Treatment of an Angry Man

In my clinical practice, I have found Binswanger's view of symptoms being the result of responsibility avoidance largely true. The case of a man I'll call Dominick is illustrative. Dominick entered therapy at age fifty, complaining of extreme anger, related to his dismissal, *ten years* earlier from his middle management job with a large corporation. He had been in therapy previously but nothing relieved that anger.

His background revealed that he had been severely traumatized in childhood by his parents' frequent and violent arguments, which were usually about money. His most pointed memory was of hiding under a table at about age four during a particularly violent argument. His parents were screaming and throwing things until finally, the police came. The argument was about money and Dominick made a vow to himself never to get married until he had enough money so he wouldn't have to argue about it. Years later, he streamlined his solution into a philosophy of diligence and hard work, with the goal of landing a secure middle management job in a large corporation. Although he dated many women, marriage was unimportant and out of the question until he had the right, secure job.

When he was in his late thirties, still single, he landed a job with a proper company and got ready to move up high enough to feel secure. He worked very hard to implement his ideas and save money for the company. He even went so far as to criticize secretaries who spent too much time on the phone. He felt he was the complete, hard working, company man who should be rewarded with promotions. Instead, he had much conflict with other employees and with his superiors. This led to a chain of events wherein his supervisors, who in his eyes had not treated him right, dismissed him from his position.

His reaction to being fired was intense rage. He tried to defend himself verbally, but got nowhere. He had to use all his effort and self control to keep himself from physically harming his supervisors whom he blamed completely for unfairly firing such a dedicated, hard worker. He then spent many months looking for the right job with the right company but always settled for inferior positions with smaller companies. The more time passed, the more he blamed and hated his supervisors. He felt *they* had cost him his only chance at security and happiness. His only regret was that he didn't attack them and beat them within an inch of their lives.

Talking about it didn't help. As Marks and Tavris say, it only made him angrier. He wrote a letter to vent his rage and read it to me. He wanted to mail it. I suggested that mailing it might wind up with him in jail. Perhaps he could find some other way of viewing what had happened to him, without telling them how much they had hurt him. Hypnosis and spiritual reframing provided some relief, but the anger kept coming back, even when he tried to tell himself that the supervisors were actors in a melodramatic play he was writing. Finally, he brought in an evaluation letter that was written about him a few months before he was fired. The letter indicated that he had a great deal of trouble getting along with his co workers and in doing the tasks his supervisors defined as important. Instead, he did what he thought was best, choosing to spend time on tasks he thought were valuable.

We went over the letter point by point. Clearly, he was not listening to his supervisors' criticisms. Then and now, he was right and they were idiots. Gradually, he was forced to admit that his ideas about how to do his job were not necessarily the right way to go if he wanted to get ahead in this organization. Had he listened to the criticism and made some adjustments, he would not have gotten fired. Though his supervisors were rather nasty and insensitive, he still would have probably kept his job if he listened to what they were saying and changed his approach to the job. He stopped blaming them for firing him and *took responsibility* for what happened. He left the office in a daze.

He returned a week later to report that he felt much better, though he didn't really know why. He still disliked the former supervisors but his anger was reduced considerably since he had accepted at least part of the responsibility for getting fired. He is now feeling like "there may be something else in life besides hard work," and is looking forward to living a happier, more balanced and responsible life.

If you have a chronic anger problem. It would be a good idea to look at it through the lens of responsibility avoidance. The simple act of accepting your role in creating what happens to you will often relieve bad feelings. In addition, hypnosis and prayer can do a lot to speed up the responsibility taking process. The following is a self hypnotic trance for those who seriously want to take responsibility for their lives.

Self-Hypnotic Exercise for Taking Responsibility

Take some time for yourself now, letting your body relax as you just follow your breathing. Whenever you are ready to go into the deepest trance you have ever been in, allow your eyes to close...(let one minute pass). There is nothing you have to do right now...you can just rest here right now and let your conscious mind drift...while your unconscious takes over...for it's your unconscious that is really in charge of healing...automatically starting the healing process as soon as a finger is cut...or the body needs help...and the same is true of psychological healing...

As soon as your unconscious accepts that you need to change your character it begins to change...taking responsibility for your choices improves your character...Is your responsibility for yourself beginning to increase yet? Are you taking more responsibility for your life yet? Can you accept that you can't control everything in your life? Can you accept that sometimes things will happen that you don't like? Do you realize that you can still be at peace when things are going against your wishes?

There are always parts of yourself that you don't like...perhaps you were told not to think, feel, behave in certain ways...so you didn't...but you began noticing these impulses, thoughts, feelings and behaviors in others and it annoyed you...the others seem to be getting away with it...it isn't fair...but you are better than that...you don't act like that...this is your shadow side...this is the part of you that you don't like to look at...your hidden thoughts, feelings, desires, your shadow side....Would you like to bring this shadow part of you into the light?? Can you see now that you have thoughts, feelings and desires that you are ashamed of? Can you see that much of what annoys you in others, is behavior that you don't allow in yourself?

Are you willing to admit that you have the potential to think, feel and do almost anything? Are you willing to take responsibility for even your hidden thoughts, feelings and desires as they arise?

If you are ready to own your shadow...and if it's all right with your unconscious...you can do so, NOW !!!!!! As soon as you see that you have hidden thoughts and feelings, you can take responsibility for them, Can you see that you could be obnoxious too...You could be the way your enemy is too......You may not want to be that way, You may even fear being that way..., but you have the potential...

Imagine now someone you dislike...imagine them doing things that annoy you...now recognize why you are annoyed...that's right it's because of your shadow...How did you learn not to be that way?...Who told you not to be that way? Once you understand how you came to dislike that sort of behavior, you can tolerate it...It's not the other person who is upsetting you...It's your own fear that you could be like that...that is what creates your shadow...and you can own your own shadow thoughts and feelings now...If you can do that, you can visualize yourself forgiving the other person...now feel how good it feels to accept all potential behavior in yourself...now see how free you are to make good responsible choices for yourself...finally, see yourself accepting any and all results of your choices...See how good it feels to surrender your need to control everything...you no longer need to be unaware of unacceptable impulses and desires...you are free...responsibility has led you to freedom...You may now take responsibility for all your thoughts and desires, for all your decisions, for all your actions...consulting with your Higher Self before each action...creating a healing alliance with your Higher Self...praying from the point of view of the Higher Self...making choices from the point of view of the greatest good for the most people....Remember to thank God or your Higher Power for giving you the strength and insight to do this work....to take so much responsibility for your life...You may find yourself repeating the prayer, "thank you God for helping me to take maximum responsibility for my thoughts, feelings and behavior...and as soon as that sense of responsibility and the freedom it leads to is accepted by your unconscious, you can slowly open your eyes and come back to the room, feeling good...much more able to own your own shadow feelings and take responsibility for your thoughts, feelings, behavior and decisions.

Chapter Eleven

Praying For Others Helps Us Too

Praying for others indicates our development of maturity. We are no longer just concerned with ourselves, but with the welfare of others. So called prayers of intercession have been practiced for thousands of years, usually in time of great stress such as serious illness. The first step in praying for others is, of course, the willingness to set aside personal concerns and devote time for the good of the other. The second step is a lot less obvious, because we don't know what is in the best interest of the other. If the prayed for person is extremely ill, should we pray for recovery (which may seem unlikely) or for a merciful end to the person's life? If the prayed for person is less ill and likely to recover but suffering a great deal, do we pray for speedy recovery? For less suffering, or for something else? If the person is in serious financial difficulty, do we pray for money? For a change in circumstances? For a new opportunity? These difficult questions require delving more deeply into the possible workings of prayers of intercession. Only then can we decide whether or not to intercede with prayer and how to do so.

Non-Local Mind

Non local mind is a generic term, invented by physicists and utilized most recently by Dr. Larry Dossey to explain the healing power of intercessory prayer. Dr. Dossey has written many books on the subject including, *Healing Words, Prayer is Good Medicine* and *Be Careful What You Pray For: You May Get It.* According to Dossey, prayers work because all minds are joined at the deepest level. This level of mind is called non-local mind because it is everywhere-not in a single locality. Prayer is seen as a joining in this non-local mind with a loving, healing intent. Before examining Dossey's work in detail, however, it will be useful to look at a several earlier attempts at explaining prayerful healing, the Marquis de Puysegur, P.P. Quimby and the work of a man whose work has been forgotten by time, Thompson Jay Hudson.

The Marquis de Puysegur

Armand Marie Jaques de Chastenet was the full name of the Marquis de Puysegur. In his younger years he was an artillery officer from a prominent family. In his thirties, however, he became interested in Mesmerism and healing through what was then called animal magnetism. He studied magnetic healing with Mesmer and had many remarkable cures. Eventually though, he developed his own theory of healing which was markedly different than Mesmer's theory.

Mesmer thought that there was a universal magnetic fluid in all living things. The magnetist healed by moving the fluid by an act of will and through "magnetic passes." Mesmer felt that this led to a crisis (a form of convulsion) which then led to healing. According to Mesmer, this was entirely a physical process.

Puysegur felt that healing was primarily a psychological process provoked by the will of the magnetist, in close *rapport* with the subject. He found that a physical crisis was neither inevitable or healing. Instead, he noticed that his subjects went into a deep somnambulistic trance, akin to the sleepwalking state. When his subjects went into this deep trance-like sleep, they had a different sort of consciousness than their usual personality. This unusual form of consciousness was often followed by a physical cure.

Puysegur emphasized that the good will and intentions of the magnetizer were essential because of the close rapport with the subject. He found that while in somnambulistic trance, his subjects were able to hear and obey the magnetist's thoughts (clairvoyance), diagnose illnesses, prescribe treatments for their illness, and develop complete amnesia once awakened. In short, Puysegur felt that healing resulted through the continuous flow of love and good will to the subject. The somnambulistic state (later called hypnosis) promoted the communication of this love and good will. Puysegur did not implore God to heal the subject, thus, his brand of mesmerism should not technically be called prayer. Yet, he was interceding with love, which is the essence of spiritual healing. It remained for later theorists and practitioners to redefine mesmerism as a spiritual process, akin to intercessory prayer.

In the 1780s the chevalier De Barberin and the Marquis de Dampierre took Mesmerism in a spiritual direction. De Barberin practiced magnetization at a distance and developed what would be called today psychic healing ability. He was consulted not only for healings but for advice on family matters, daily problems in living and metaphysical speculation on life after death. He had considerable success in all these areas. De Dampierre investigated claims of medical clairvoyance undertaken in magnetic trance and declared their validity and usefulness beyond reproach. The spiritual magnetic healing (hypnosis) movement spread all over France and even to Sweden where the Swedenborg Society began to study Mesmerism and magnetic healing.

Emmanuel Swedenborg (1688-1772) was a Swedish mystic who later influenced P.P.Quimby and the New Thought movement. Swedenborg felt that there were both good and evil spirits which secretly influenced human activities. After studying Mesmerism and magnetization, the Stockholm Swedenborg Society felt that magnetic trance enabled practitioners to contact spirits and obtain their help in healing. This was another step toward the spiritual in magnetic or hypnotic healing, leading hypnosis closer to intercessory prayer than ever before. Whether the healing agent was the soul of the hypnotist or a beneficial spirit, hypnosis was moving closer to intercessory prayer than ever before.

Quimby and the New Thought Movement

Phineas Parkhurst Quimby was a modest, self educated handyman from Belfast, Maine. He studied Mesmerism and hypnosis in the 1820s and by the 1830s cured himself of severe neurasthenia (tiredness) via self hypnosis. He eventually abandoned the hypnotic element, deciding that suggestion was enough to heal. He felt that the healing agent in all illness was the patient's belief. Later, he realized that the most healing beliefs were metaphysical and spiritual. After his death in 1866, there was much debate as to how much credit he deserved as the founder of the new thought movement. Today, most new thought philosophies including Unity, Christian Science, and Science of Mind all acknowledge Quimby's importance.

One example of Quimby's importance to the New Thought healing movement was the work of Reverend Warren Evans. Evans, who had been healed by Quimby, wrote a book called *The Mental Cure*. In this book, Evans wrote that healing was not the result of mental manipulations of thought. Rather, healing was spiritual in nature, the result of what Swedenborg called "divine influx", "love" and "the Christ."

My personal investigations into the roots of healing, prayer, spirituality and hypnosis took me through these pioneering efforts and many later new thought theorists, including Myrtle and Charles Fillmore (Unity School), Ernest Holmes (Science of Mind) and Emmet Fox. Though these schools of healing and spirituality all seemed related to hypnosis, prayer and healing, the connections all came together through a man whose work was popular in its time but has been forgotten today.

Is Hypnosis a Form of Prayer?

Browsing in a used bookstore one day in Seattle, Washington, when I came across a little book with a curious title, *The Law Of Psychic Phenomena: A Working Hypothesis For The Systematic Study Of Hypnotism, Spiritism, Mental Therapeutics Etc.* by Thompson Jay Hudson, published in 1893. Despite the wordy title and the somewhat archaic language, the book proved fascinating, and has been of incredible importance to me in my personal search to integrate hypnosis and prayer into the healing psychotherapeutic work that I do.

Hudson's theory is that we all possess two minds which he terms the *objective* and *subjective* minds. Today we would be more likely to call them the conscious and unconscious mind. The objective mind is seen as that part of us that governs our everyday external actions. It is the part of us of which we are most aware that operates through the physical senses, is our guide in our struggle with the material environment and has as its highest function, reasoning. The subjective mind is aware of its environment by a sixth sense, intuition. It is the seat of the emotions and the storehouse of memory. It performs its highest functions when the objective mind is suspended by deep sleep, somnambulistic hypnosis or meditation. It can leave the body, travel any distance and gather remote information. It is "*a distinct entity, possessing independent powers and functions, having a mental organization of it's own, and being capable of sustaining an existence independently of the body. In other words, it is the soul.*" (Hudson 1893 p30)

Hudson's hypnotic healing techniques are based upon completely silencing the objective mind (or ego) with all its reasoning and skepticism, and then implanting healing suggestions directly into the subjective mind (or soul). The soul, he asserts, is completely open to anything suggested. Further, it is the soul which "has absolute control of the functions, conditions and sensations of the body." (Ibid, p. 151) As proof of this statement he refers to hypnotic phenomena such as anesthesia, as well as hypnotic production of physical symptoms (which had already been amply demonstrated by that time). If the soul controls the body, he reasoned, then another person could positively influence a diseased body by influencing the subjective mind (soul) of the sick person.

According to Hudson, this healing would be accomplished as long as two conditions were present. First, the healer needs absolute faith in his ability. Second, the healer must still his own conscious mind through self hypnosis or sleep. Let us examine each of these factors in turn.

Hudson begins his examination of the importance of faith with Jesus Christ's admonition to his disciples who were complaining to him about the lessening of their healing powers. "Oh ye of little faith," he retorted-regarding faith thus, as an essential element in healing. Hudson feels that is *why* faith is so essential and will not be understood until "we are able to fathom the ultimate cause of all things." (Hudson, 1897 p. 155) Hudson regards the skeptical attitude of the conscious (objective) mind to be the single greatest deterrent to healing. The cure always requires *faith*. His reasoning is that the subjective (unconscious) mind follows the suggestions of its own objective mind as well as the suggestions of others. "The faith required for therapeutic purposes is a purely *subjective* faith, and is attainable upon the cessation of active opposition on the part of the objective mind." (Hudson, 1897, p. 156) The objective mind here sounds curiously like a nineteenth-century version of the troublesome ego that *A Course in Miracles* warns us about.

Hudson also thought that the ego got in the way of healing. His way of dealing with the troublesome ego was to create "perfect passivity" on the part of the patient. The patient would then use auto-suggestion (affirmative prayer) or the suggestion of another (intercession). It is nice, he says, to have the conscious mind in agreement, but not necessary. He uses Christian Science healings as evidence for his theory.

Although he finds Christian Science logic absurd, he nevertheless asserts that there are many healings after a half-hour or so of Christian Science prayer treatment (which denies the reality of the body and affirms perfect health).

In order to create the best possible conditions for healing, he suggests that both the patient *and the healer* be hypnotized, with the healer *affirming* perfect health through statements which we might call intercessory prayer. He feels that this telepathically impresses the soul or subjective mind of the patient, producing the healing. Many healers tell their patients that faith on their part is not necessary. He considers this a trick to silence the skeptical conscious mind, opening the way for the more gullible faith of the unconscious. He recommends following Jesus and proclaiming the importance of faith, though it appears that the faith of the unconscious mind is of primary importance. At any rate, the conscious mind must be quieted to allow the healing to take place in the unconscious. "Ye shall know the truth and the truth shall set you free." But the truth must be known and grasped by the *unconscious*. This is another way of saying that the ego must get quiet and join with the Higher Self (which is part of the unconscious) for the truth that *all is one* to heal the mind and the body.

If we leap forward to the pioneering hypnotic work of Dr. Milton Erickson (1930s-1981), we can see why his techniques were so successful and rapidly gaining popularity today. Of course, Erickson didn't call it prayer, he called it hypnosis, but the principles are the same. Erickson said that there were five steps to the hypnotic process: *fixating* attention, *depotentiating* (quieting) the conscious mind, *promoting* the unconscious search, the post hypnotic *suggestion*, and the post hypnotic *response*.

Four of these five steps can easily be translated into Hudson's language. Hudson might say: *fixate* attention via rapport, *quiet* the objective mind via hypnosis or sleep, *send* healing messages to the unconscious verbally and by telepathy with complete faith in their efficacy, and expect a post hypnotic *response* of healing. The only step he leaves out is, promoting the unconscious search for the answer. This omission results from his nineteenth century view that the answer should be provided as a command to heal. Since the prevailing belief was that the subjective mind always followed orders, Hudson felt the command would work.

Both Erickson and Hudson felt that healing is promoted by the patient and the healer both going into trance. Hudson felt that this enabled two subjective minds to connect in complete faith, resulting in healing. This joining of minds actually replaces the need for Erickson's third step, the unconscious search for solution. *The solution is the joining of minds.* Erickson felt that he was at his most creative while in trance and thereby most able to stimulate the unconscious of the patient to utilize its resources to heal himself. Erickson was decidedly non-mystical in his approach, yet his five step hypnotic process was remarkably similar to that of the mystic, Hudson.

I believe that Dossey's concept of non-local mind connects these two approaches and improves upon them. Let us imagine changing Hudson's mystical, hypnotic language and Erickson's pragmatic, psychological language to the language of intercessory prayer. Step one would be the same, except that in the *physical absence of the patient*, one might fixate attention on prayer for that patient. Step two would be to *quiet* the conscious mind by contacting the Higher Power or non-local mind, bypassing the conscious mind. Step three would be an open ended suggestion for the Higher Power to stimulate the lower unconscious to do whatever work is necessary for the healing to take place. Step four would be the post hypnotic suggestion in the form of a *non-directive* prayer, uniting your unconscious with the patient's unconscious, affirming perfect love, peace and health for both of you. Step five would be awaiting the healing result with perfect faith and watching for its material manifestation. It is the nature of non-local mind that ties this whole healing process together. Note the practitioner begins by being directive and ends by being non directive, simply joining minds in a sort of "sea of love", that Dossey terms, *non-local mind.*

This process is echoed by Dr. Larry Le Shan and Dr. Joyce Goodrich's three step approach to healing through focused meditation. Step one is centering, moving into the meditative state through any comfortable method. Step two is focusing on the patient through gently and lovingly joining the consciousness of the patient (this is often done by gazing at a picture of the patient). Step three is a complete letting go of the laws of cause and effect, watching your imagery non-judgmentally, with compassion, letting it go where it may. The technique is greatly enhanced by practice and the development of faith by the healer. Once again we see many similarities to the models of Hudson, Erickson and Dossey.

Evidence Is Mounting

One might wonder what evidence there is for the efficacy of such methods. How often do these techniques work? How often don't they work? What are the conditions under which they work the best? What are the conditions causing them not to work at times? We begin with Hudson's breakthroughs one hundred years ago.

Hudson's favorite technique involved both the healer and the healee to be asleep. He felt this was the state of "perfect passivity" in which the subjective mind of the healer could influence the subjective mind of the patient. He suggested that the healer use affirmations powered by an act of will toward the patient. For example he would affirm several times as he fell asleep: *"the patient is healing, the patient is healing, the patient is healed while I sleep tonight, my subjective mind is traveling to see this patient and all night it will continue to impress his subjective mind with healing thoughts and energy...the patient is healed, the patient is healed, the patient is healed.*" Then he would fall asleep convinced that his subjective mind would take over.

His results were phenomenal. He states, that "over one hundred experiments have been made by the writer and one or two others to whom he has confided his theory, without a single failure. *Some very striking cures have been effected...The diseases thus far successfully treated by this process have been rheumatism, neuralgia, dyspepsia, bowel complaint, sick headache, torpidity of the liver, chronic bronchitis, partial paralysis, pen paralysis and strabismus. One fact of peculiar significance with the case of rheumatism is that the patient was one thousand miles distant when the cure was performed. Others have been successfully treated at distances varying from one to three hundred miles.*" (Ibid, p.194-5) Though some may doubt the scientific rigor of the reporting, the writer provides much anecdotal evidence for the efficacy of his method. Hudson seemed to think that the healer's subjective mind sends healing commands to the sick person's subjective mind. Distance doesn't seem to matter. These are very interesting early reports of non-local healing.

Dossey has reported that similar research was done in the 1920's in Russia by Bekhterev and DeSoille of the Commission for the Study of Mental Suggestion. Vasiliev, who was a central researcher on the commission, believed that Desoille's idea of suggestions made from one person's unconscious to another person's unconscious was quite viable. Even Freud believed that communication between people could take place entirely on the unconscious level. He did not, however, think of using this communicative power for purposeful healing purposes.

It remained for Dossey, writing one hundred years later to develop the concept of non-local mind to explain the same phenomena that Hudson observed. Dossey, in 1993, made the following hypothesis in response to the scientific research on prayer: There is a transcendent force in the universe called by physicists non-local mind. Information in such a world is not sent, it exists everywhere at once.

When loving intent toward healing is present, the natural tendency is to produce healing in the intended. Distance doesn't matter since the nature of consciousness is non-local and the information needed for healing is everywhere. All individual minds are really joined by non-local mind. Nothing needs to be "sent", since all minds are joined at the deepest level.

Dossey's work clearly indicates that much progress in non-local healing has been made since the time of Hudson. Whereas Hudson advocates using the will to *send* specific healing messages, Dossey advocates a non-directive, "Thy will be done" sort of prayer. His feeling is that in "a non-local world, it seems impossible that a previously thought out message could be sent from one locality to another. In fact one can never know ahead of time what these instantly correlated changes between distant entities will be; it is only in retrospect that we know they have taken place by reading a record of some sort that tells us what happened." (Dossey 1993, p.85)

From Dossey's point of view, Hudson's hypnotic commands for healing might have been too specific. Hudson's ideas do have a curiously nineteenth century flavor. He would make the patient completely passive and then *command* him to heal. Yet, he seems to be coming from a very loving place in ordering his sick subjects to heal. He writes, "Each one has it in his power to alleviate the sufferings of his neighbor, his friend or the stranger within his gates; but his compensation must consist in the consciousness of doing good, and in the hope of that reward promised by the Master to those who do their alms in secret." (Ibid p. 196) In other words he was advocating the same sort of selfless intercessory prayer currently being written about by Dossey, Le Shan and Goodrich. The only difference is in the exact form of the prayers.

Hudson advocated direct prayers from one person's unconscious to the other's. Dossey and Le Shan advocate a non-directive, loving sort of prayer for the best thing to happen in this particular circumstance. Hudson was right about the connection needing to be made from one unconscious mind to another, bypassing the conscious skepticism that is frequently present. Dossey and Le Shan seem to be right in being non-directive. All current prayer research indicates that both directive and non-directive prayers "work." However, non-directive prayer seems to work better. For a detailed account of the research see Dossey (1993), Menahem (1995) or the three volume set of prayer research put out by the National Institute of Health Care Research in Rockville, Maryland.

In addition to working better, the non-directive prayers are more ethical and make more sense. They are more ethical because no one could argue or have any problem with the "best thing happening for all concerned." They are more logical because they include the element of humility. It is impossible to use one's ego to determine what is best for oneself, let alone another. This way, the particular goal and means are turned over to the transcendent aspect of God (non-local mind). The book of Job is illustrative here.

In the biblical book of Job, God and Satan make a bet. Satan says that Job, a very pious, spiritual person, will curse God if enough bad things happen to him. God says Job will remain true to him. Despite his goodness, things begin to fall apart for Job. He loses his flocks, his wife, and his children. He becomes very ill with painful boils. His friends try to tell him that he must have done something wrong to deserve this. He says, "No, I did nothing wrong ! Bad things are indeed happening to a good person." Job curses the day he was born, but will not curse God. Finally, Job meets God and angrily complains that he did nothing to deserve all this pain. God tells him that when he (Job) creates a world, he can come back and complain. Until then, he should go along with God's program. Job complies and all of his wealth is restored. He even gets a new family!

What does all this have to do with prayer? It is not our place really to tell the universe, non-local mind or God what to do and how to do it. Non-directive prayer, especially as an intercession for someone else accomplishes a lot without the sin of hubris (spiritual pride). We are expressing our love, compassion and concern through the prayers. This is probably one of the keys to what the Higher Power wants of us. Yet, we are respectful of the "mysterium tremendum," the baffling transpersonal aspect of life. We are not using our puny conscious ego to order or command anything—even healing. We are releasing the seeming problem of sickness and suffering to the unconscious mind where God resides. We are willing to do our part and let go and let God do the rest in the way that He deems fit. Within this wider context, all prayers for healing are answered. Sometimes, as the Buddhists say, "death is the answer." Other times there are miraculous recoveries. Still other times lives are extended with emotional healing. We provide the non-directive prayers to non-local mind. God provides the answers, through the medium of non-local mind. We must learn to recognize the answers to our prayers—even those we don't like.

Chapter Twelve

Advancing Further By Praising God

God is both immanent and transcendent. This basic truth is espoused by both Judaism and Christianity as well as being implied by most other religions. Unfortunately, this truth is frequently ignored or misunderstood. It means simply that there is a universal intelligence operating both within each human being and beyond complete human understanding. Understanding this concept is not promoted by the prevalent view of God in Western religion, which is the concept of God as a king, an ego-centered point of view. In this view, God is seen as outside human beings, more powerful than any person and controlling everything. Staying at this level does not promote awe or adoration except in the sense of fear. This is not unlike our early childhood view of a powerful parent. We better be good or else we will be punished. Fear of God, however, is even worse than fear of a parent: we might be able to fool a parent and get away with a transgression, whereas we can't fool God the king.

If we take this concept seriously, we will be very afraid of doing anything wrong, because God will know about it and punish us. We will also feel guilty about doing anything wrong, and feel that we deserve punishment. There is much talk in religion of how we *should* fear God and I think this misconception of God as a vengeful parent is the reason for the fear. If we have such fear, we might engage in praising God with prayers of adoration for the wrong reason: to placate an angry parental God.

Some people are turned off to religion and God because of the external king metaphor. They see too much suffering to feel God is a *loving* powerful deity. Such suffering often leads to skepticism and disbelief in any God. This agnostic or atheistic view of life certainly would not lead to prayers of adoration. A materialist might say, "who or what are you adoring? There is no evidence of a caring, kingly God to love or pray to. Even if there were such a God, why would he or she want to be adored by prayer." Such a God could be seen as no better than a narcissistic person. I admit to having this thought in my youth.

The Spiritual impulse is a strong one, however, so some people continue searching for some sort of God to believe in. Thus, many of us become interested in Spirituality from a different point of view: the view that God is entirely internal. "New Age" thought promotes the idea of an internal God. This makes sense to many, but easily leads to confusing the ego (conscious self) with the Higher Self (unconscious). Ego inflation results if we think our conscious mind with its wishes and desires is God. This is what probably happens with the cult massacres we frequently hear about. The Dave Koresh or Jim Jones kind of leader thinks their *ego is* God and tries to rule everyone. Since ego-inflated leaders are unstable and deranged, their vulnerable followers end up dead! A true guru or avatar would not claim they are God except in the sense that everyone is God.

This leads us back to our original statement, God is immanent and transcendent. Those of us who have experienced the first three stages of the theology to be outlined in this chapter have realized that God is much more than an external King. We also know that our ego is not God. The missing piece is the transcendent aspect of God. We know that God is within us, but there is also something beyond us with which we can and should connect with. As we continue our search for God, this transcendent element begins to become more alluring. Our spiritual search is no longer about a desire to control events or dominate others. We realize that the elusive, loving, mysterious, powerful aspect of the transcendent God is really in charge of our individual lives and of life in general. The awe we feel is not fear, it is reverence. We desire to pray with adoration because it *feels right*. It is not a means of control. It is not even a means of healing our bodies or anyone else's body. It is the natural thing to do and may result in the healing of our soul. Healing the soul is reconnecting with the transcendent.

Prayers of adoration spring from deep inside the human soul. I am referring here to praying to God with all one's heart and soul, not lip service, mechanical prayers. In Judaism, it is easy to chant the *sh'ma* (Hear O Israel, the Lord our God, the Lord is One) or the *Amidah* which is full of adoration without thinking or feeling anything. I believe such prayers miss the mark. I feel it is better to say a one line prayer with intense feeling than to race through long prayers by rote. This concept, called *kavannah* in Judaism is vital to really practicing prayers of adoration.

Professor Arthur Freeman of Moravian Theological Seminary warns us not to identify God with the world. He quotes 20th century mystic Simone Weil: "God in love created the world and then gave it it's freedom. It now functions by it's own laws, by necessity, by what she calls gravity. God can then penetrate the world by grace and may be discovered by what one finds in it (as it's creator) but is not to be identified with it." (Freeman, 1998, p.8) Thus, God is much more than just the world or nature. God is more even than the universe. In that sense God is mysterious, powerful and transcendent. This mysterious element inspires us to pray adoringly. I believe such prayers of adoration have an effect on God and an effect on us. We don't understand the effect of such prayers and don't pray for the effect. We do it out of love. It is a recognition of what really *is*.

Huxley's View of Adoration

Aldous Huxley felt that adoration was the same as intercession with a different object. He stated: "Intercession then, is at once the means to, and the expression of love for one's neighbor. And in the same way adoration is the means to, and the expression of, the love of God-a love that finds it's consummation in the unitive knowledge of the Godhead which is the fruit of contemplation." (Huxley, 1944 p.223) He quotes Bourgoing as saying, "The aim and end of prayer is to revere, recognize and adore the sovereign majesty of God, through what He is in Himself rather than what He is in regard to us, and rather to love his goodness by the love of that goodness itself than for what it sends us." (Ibid p.223)

This short quote includes many important elements in our search to understand the power of prayers of adoration. First, we need to honor the greatness of God over that conscious portion of ourselves (ego) that we usually think of as all we are. Second we need to love God regardless of what he might do for us. Third, we need to love God's goodness for itself, unattached to any results, favors or powers it might bring us. Thus, prayers of adoration help us to surrender to the transcendent God—who is in charge anyway. It is what Washburn suggests we do through meditation: yield to the Ground of Being.

Immanuel Kant, the philosopher, wrote that God, himself, was unknowable. Huxley agrees, but only for minds that have not yet come to enlightenment and deliverance. To the enlightened mind, there is no separate selfhood to "obscure and refract" the experience of God. Many people commit to God and try to adore him but still yearn for glory and grandiosity for themselves. This search for glory, so aptly described by psychiatrist Karen Horney in the 1940s, is a result of childhood love deficits. The parents were too self absorbed to love the child unselfishly. This narcissistic self-absorption is so prevalent in our time that it is the norm. So many Spiritual seekers need help overcoming their need for grandiosity. Prayers of adoration help us to transcend our egocentricity and need for glory. It is not our ego self that is great, it is our God Self, *especially the transcendent element.*

Huxley quotes St. Anselm: "Lord, teach me to seek thee and reveal thyself to me when I seek thee. For I cannot seek thee except thou teach me, nor find Thee except thou reveal Thyself." (Ibid p.224) This is a prayer of surrender and adoration. It recognizes that we need to turn to God to overcome the allure of the tricky ego. As we adore God, and surrender, we are helped to get to the next step of spiritual development.

Goldsmith's View of Adoration

Joel Goldsmith was a firm believer that we should never ask God for things, nor should we tell God anything. In his view our prayers should be completely adoring. We should acknowledge God by realizing;

"God, Thou art the infinite intelligence, which hast created this entire universe, the Intelligence that knows how to govern it without any help from me. forgive me father if I have ever told thee what I need or what my family or nation needs. Father, forgive me every time I have lifted up my eyes in the hope that thou wouldst serve me. Let me understand that I was created in Thy image and likeness to show forth Thy glory. The heavens declare the glory of God; the earth shows forth His bounty."

Goldsmith, 1992, p. 27

Goldsmith was of the opinion that God must be totally trusted to act in the interests of all creatures. Prayer, according to Goldsmith is an affirmation of trust and awe.

Wilber's View

Transpersonal theorist Ken Wilber posits ten stages of human psychological development. The first six stages are essentially psychological and the aim is to develop a strong independent ego. The next three stages involve developing the spiritual insight necessary to *let go of the ego* with it's inherent grandiosity. This is total surrender of the ego to God. The final step is full Self-realization, by the illumination of seeing fully that the ego is no longer needed. This has been called many names including *satori*, but the phrase *Cosmic Consciousness*, coined in 1900, by a Canadian physician named Bucke will suffice. Prayers of adoration are part of the path to cosmic consciousness.

Huxley concludes, "Adoration is an activity of the loving but still separate individuality. Contemplation is the state of union with the divine Ground of all Being. The highest prayer is the most passive. Inevitably; for the less there is of self, the more there is of God. That is why the path to passive or infused contemplation is so hard and, for many, so painful-a passage through successive or simultaneous dark nights, in which the pilgrim must die to the life of sense as an end in itself, to the life of private and even of traditionally hallowed thinking and believing and finally to the deep source of all ignorance and evil, the life of the separate, individualized will." (Ibid p.227) This curious goal is reachable via the fourth type of prayer, meditation, to which we now turn.

CHAPTER THIRTEEN

MEDITATION: THE HIGHEST FORM OF PRAYER

Meditation is the highest form of prayer. This does not mean that it is better than any other form. Nor does it mean we should skip the other forms. It simply means that meditation is a natural occurrence as our prayer life evolves. Through practicing other types of prayer, or simply through life experience, our God concept evolves (king, atheism, Self) until we have the desire to meditate. Our spiritual growth leads to our being pulled by the "oneness" of God to give up our individuality and to experience a merger. Just as there are processes of physical and psychological development, there are processes of spiritual and prayer development in our Earthly life. When we begin to sense that there is an essential unity between us and God, we want to *feel it*. At this point meditation is a natural form of prayer to use. It can be used in combination with other forms or it may be used alone.

Meditation: The Royal Road to the Unconscious

Michael Washburn paraphrases Freud by calling meditation, not dreams, the "royal road" to the unconscious. He does not deny that dreams can uncover the unconscious, he just feels that meditation is a more consistent, "user friendly," path. In Washburn's opinion, meditation, though less spectacular than hypnosis or drugs in accessing the

152

unconscious, is a "permanent linkage between conscious and unconscious systems." (Washburn, 1988, p.140)

In explaining meditation, he uses the metaphor of a fisherman: Hypnosis and drug interventions are like a fisherman plunging himself into the water to catch a fish. On the other hand, dream analysis and Jung's active imagination are too sedate. They are like the fisherman who sticks too close to shore. Meditation is just right. "It becomes more than just a connection (between the conscious and unconscious); it becomes a unifying synthesis of (what were) conscious and unconscious systems." (Ibid p.141)

The Trivialization of Meditation

American pop culture has led to a misconception of what meditation is. In the 1970s many researchers of the physical benefits of meditation such as Benson and Carrington published their results. They placed so much emphasis on the physical benefits of anxiety reduction, mood elevation, blood pressure reduction etc. that many people overlooked the fact that meditation is usually thought of as a *Spiritual* discipline. Meditation was seen as merely another psychological technique to "feel better." In actuality, meditation is primarily a spiritual technique, a form of prayer, to heal the soul. It just so happens that as we heal the soul we also often heal at the "lower" physical and psychological levels.

On the other end of the spectrum, religious fundamentalists have decried meditation as a tool of the devil gleaned from "godless" Eastern religions. Nothing could be further from the truth. Washburn declares that prayer is a form of meditation. I think the reverse is true, meditation is a form of prayer *that recognizes the oneness of all Being and makes no effort to control God or Being*. Thus, we have moved one step beyond adoration. There is no longer even any external object (an anthropomorphic God) to adore. Rather, through meditation, we are tuning into and merging with the nature of God and of humankind. As we link up, we feel the love, peace and lightness of Being, truly Cosmic Consciousness. Those are the rewards of good meditative moments. During the difficult meditative moments, we need the strength and equanimity to accept and work with what we can't immediately change. As Victor Frankl said, we can always change our attitude. As *A Course In Miracles* says, "You could choose peace. instead of this (upset, anger etc.)."

Concentrative Meditation

Washburn splits meditation into two major groups, concentrative and receptive. There are many differences between them but, most importantly, the *similarity* is that both forms of meditation are "practices of pure steadfast attention." Concentrative meditation usually involves the use of a "mantra" or phrase that is repeated over and over in the mind. This approach was first popularized in this country by the "Transcendental Meditation (TM)" movement, led by the Maharishi Mahesh Yogi in the 1970s.

TM requires meeting with a teacher several times to learn the basics and be given a mantra, specifically chosen for each student. The mantra is usually a Sanskrit word, chosen more for its sound than for it's meaning and the mantra word must remain a secret. Students are taught to meditate for 20 minutes, twice a day, repeating the mantra, in a melodious way, silently. If the mind wanders off the mantra, you just return to the mantra. Diligent practice leads one to a much greater stage of peace and harmony with ones world. The popularization of TM was a big step in moving the formerly mystical technique into mainstream western culture. The emphasis on physical and psychological effects helped meditation gain acceptance in the West. If it had been presented as primarily spiritual, I don't think it would have caught on.

Many thousand people have learned and still practice TM. Many psychotherapists have utilized it. In 1977, psychologist Patricia Carrington wrote a book called *Freedom in Meditation*, outlining all the benefits and encouraging the spread of meditation. She essentially taught concentrative meditation as the TM people did with much less ceremony and secrecy. The mantra was chosen from a list for its intuitive appeal and the word was not a secret, but a tool for psychological growth. People gathered in groups and were taught the essentials. The attitude taught was a non-striving, acceptance of whatever came up during the twice daily practice periods. In addition, students were taught to say, "here goes nothing," before starting, removing the goal directed idea of "I must get it right and feel great afterwards." I also cultivate this non-striving, non-goal directed attitude when teaching people meditation. The only goal is to get the person to commit to *doing* the meditation daily. The benefits happen as side effects. Carrington's book helped popularize and demystify concentrative meditation.

Dr. Herb Benson popularized and demystified concentrative meditation even further, through his best selling book, *The Relaxation Response*. Dr. Benson discovered that his patients had immense physical and psychological benefit when they meditated consistently using what he termed any nonsensical word. The nonsense word he recommended was, "One." *The Relaxation Response* alerted many people to the benefits of meditating. Several years later, Benson realized that "One" was not a nonsense word, it related to the oneness of the universe. Further, in *Beyond The Relaxation Response*, he stated that the mantra was especially potent if it was *meaningful* to the meditator. It was the job of the meditation teacher or therapist to help the student (patient) develop a meaningful mantra, utilizing the existing belief system.

In Benson's most recent book, *Timeless Healing*, he observes that we are "hard wired for God." This means that meditating with a meaningful mantra activates a biological imperative. It seems we are *supposed* to seek God through meditation. The benefits, on all levels, occur because we are doing the right thing—biologically as well as psychologically and spiritually. The way to promote well being and species survival, says Benson, is concentrative meditation with a meaningful mantra.

Not all forms of concentrative meditation involve the use of mantras. Christmas Humphreys, in his book, *Concentration and Meditation*, feels that learning to concentrate on an object is only a preparation for meditation, which can be focusing on an idea. Dr. Robert Leichtman, in his book, *Active Meditation*, recommends using positive words, e.g. wisdom, compassion as the mantras. He feels that this active *pointing* toward a goal, with excellent concentration, is much more beneficial than merely pure absorption. This, however, is a minority view. Most teachers of concentrative meditation emphasize the *importance of absorption*. The ancient Hindu mystic, Patanjali, divided concentrative meditations into three stages: concentration, meditation, and absorption. To Patanjali, all three stages were important, though it was only in the third stage that the seeker realizes the true oneness of all things, gaining maximal benefit from the meditation.

Receptive Meditation

Washburn states, "Receptive meditation is the practice of sustained, nonselective alertness. In practicing receptive meditation, the meditator maintains the stance of an open and unmoving witness. Whatever emerges in or before the mind is observed crisply but not in any way acted upon or reacted to. The images, feelings and thoughts that present themselves to consciousness are witnessed uninterruptedly, and with full consciousness, but without in any way being engaged." (Washburn, 1988, pp141-2.)

Receptive meditation has gained popularity recently through the work of Jon Kabat-Zinn (*Full Catastrophe Living, Wherever You Go, There You Are*), Jack Kornfield (*A Path With Heart*) Stephen Levine (*A Gradual Awakening*) and others. All these writers espouse a form of insight (vipassana) meditation. Through a non attached, non-judgmental watching, insight into the true nature of reality begins to dawn.

For Washburn, as well as these many other authors, meditation is the practice that opens up the mental ego (conscious mind) to the unconscious. I must emphasize that meditation opens the ego to *all* levels of the unconscious, the personal unconscious as well as the superconscious. Thus, it undoes the original repression of early adulthood. Original repression was necessary at that time, but by middle age it has outlived it's usefulness. The purpose of meditation is to refocus attention on the unconscious.

In receptive meditation, there is an *immediate awareness* of the mental chatter of the ego, which is just observed silently until it begins to dissipate. At this point, repressed memories and feelings may arise which can be re-experienced, processed and transcended. With concentrative meditation, there is a steady movement into the superconscious section of the unconscious. This temporary merger with the superconscious, sometimes called absorption, does not bring up feelings and memories until *after* the period of meditation. In both types of meditation the essential element is demobilizing the ego. This allows the contents of the personal unconscious to well up, be re-experienced (what psychoanalysts call *abreaction*), and reintegrated. Through meditation, the unconscious becomes conscious, producing a healing.

There is, however, an added dimension beyond the healing of the traumas of the personal unconscious. That is, there is added value in the absorption in and merger with the superconscious created by concentrative meditations. This is an *experience* of oneness which demonstrates the truth that all minds are joined in oneness. According to *A Course in Miracles*, all guilt and anxiety are really caused by the illusion that separation is real. Concentrative meditation demonstrates that at the deepest level there is oneness rather than separation. *Experiencing* this oneness, even briefly, allows us to be more peaceful, kind and loving.

Meditation produces the miracle of love by enabling us to be "in the world but not of it." Thus, when meditation is practiced regularly, we are repeatedly experiencing the "truth that sets us free." I believe this is why there are so many remarkable health benefits to meditation. The stresses of repressed emotions in the personal unconscious are gradually relieved. Plus, there are regular visits to the superconscious to *feel* the way oneness feels. In this way, the problems that seem physical and psychological are cured by experiencing spiritual truth.

Hypnosis and Meditation

The first two steps of hypnosis and meditation are remarkably similar. Washburn tells us that in order to meditate we must, first, concentrate and second, demobilize the ego. Similarly, hypnotherapist Dr. Milton Erickson says the first two steps of hypnosis are fixation of attention and "depotentiating" the conscious mind. The third step of hypnosis and meditation varies. In receptive meditation, the third step is an evenly hovering, non-judgmental awareness of the unconscious material that presents itself. In concentrative meditation, the third step is a movement into superconscious absorption, without ideation or cognition. In Ericksonian hypnosis, the third step is to promote the unconscious search for emotional processing of traumas and creative solutions.

In concentrative meditation, there is no fourth step, though Washburn tells us that unconscious material may arise after the meditation. This could be a fourth step. The fourth step in receptive meditation is a continuation of non-attached, non-judgmental witnessing of repressed feelings and memories. The fourth step of Ericksonian hypnosis is the post hypnotic suggestion. This is a more active way of healing a problem, where a direct or indirect suggestion is made to solve the problem. This is more like some of the petitionary prayers mentioned earlier in the book than meditation.

The fifth step in receptive meditation is reintegration of non-egoic potentials. This is a newfound ability to think, feel and behave, now that the repressed feelings and experiences no longer have to be warded off. Plus, there is the benefit of being more open to the power of the Ground (God) now that we are more comfortable with the personal unconscious. The fifth step in concentrative meditation is also a more relaxed, open, well integrated personality, but it is due to *experiencing the transpersonal ground* (God), more than processing old emotions and memories from the personal unconscious.

The fifth step in hypnosis is the "post hypnotic response." This may be any behavioral, emotional or cognitive response to the hypnotic process and suggestion. Thus, over time, the results of hypnosis could be very similar to either type of meditation. Washburn prefers meditation to hypnosis because it is steadier and more consistent in opening up the unconscious. Actually, the processes are so similar that either one, practiced diligently could lead to ample spiritual growth.

Getting Started with Meditation

If you intuitively feel a need for meditation it is easy to get started. I usually meditate briefly with new meditators using a simple concentrative breath meditation: I instruct them to count their breaths from one to four, saying to themselves on the inhale, one, exhale ahhhhh and so on...until four then begin again. This is all to be done with no particular goal, except doing it. You cannot do it wrong (a very hard concept for most people). There are no good or bad results. All results are O.K. There is no judgment or performance.

I explain that there are many common side benefits like relaxation, stress reduction and physical well being but that this is much more than just a technique. It is a daily spiritual exercise which when practiced diligently will transform their lives. I ask each person how long he or she would like to practice daily. We start with whatever time period seems plausible and gradually work our way up to twenty minutes once or twice a day.

Finally, we set a daily time to practice, enhancing the commitment. Each week I ask about the meditations and support all efforts. I also recommend a friend who will support all efforts. I also mention possible side effects including sudden tension release and the possibility of old memories and emotions surfacing.

If requested, at some later time, I encourage different meditations that can be practiced utilizing with the same general comments about meditation. They may pick a mantra from Carrington's list, take a TM course, develop a meaningful mantra from their own belief system e.g. *shalom* for religious Jews, or pick a positive quality e.g. love, peace, wisdom and contemplate it. They may also ask a question of their Higher Self—e.g. what do I need to learn from this experience?—Then observe answers bubbling up from their unconscious. The possibilities are endless and the benefits are great.

For those who begin to take to a particular kind of meditation I recommend various books. A great place to start is Larry Le Shan's, *How To Meditate*. For those who prefer receptive meditation, the already mentioned works by Jon Kabat-Zinn and Jack Kornfield are recommended. A lot can be gained by practicing meditation on your own and augmenting it with reading material.

Should I Get a Teacher

The old saying, when the student is ready, the teacher appears is relevant. If you accidentally meet a meditation teacher, take note. He or she may be heaven sent. If you gravitate to a particular tradition, e.g. Zen Buddhist, Yoga, Vedanta; it can be invaluable to find a knowledge-able teacher and study with a class or privately. A good way to try a teacher or tradition is to go on a meditational retreat. If the experience resonates well for you, you may want to continue with that type of meditation. Check the teacher out, however, using both rational and intuitive means. If the teacher seems to live what he or she espouses and meditating with that person feels peaceful to you, you are probably on the right track.

CHAPTER FOURTEEN

MAKING YOUR LIFE A PRAYER

The more each of us turns to God through all types of prayer, the more we are aware of our thoughts, feelings and deeper Self. Part of the answer to any form of prayer is clear awareness of much more of our Self than just the ego. Prayer opens us up to our unconscious and superconscious mind. As I suggested in Chapter One, our thought processes, powered by emotions create our reality. Thus, in a sense we are informally "praying" our lives into physical form without realizing what we are doing. We are not addressing these prayers to God in a petitionary way. Yet, God is answering, because it is the nature of God to co-create our reality according to his/her laws and the individual belief systems, thoughts and feelings of each person. Co-creation is a little understood concept. When it is properly understood, we see that all is going according to God's nature and laws. *We, ourselves are love and All really is love.* However, our limited beliefs distort our loving Godly nature into Earthly lives, full of fear, guilt and suffering. The problems in living we experience are due to our unwillingness and or inability to experience our Godly loving nature, where all is love and peace. Our chaotic lives are due to our fearful egoic belief system. That is our contribution toward co-creation. As long as we have a fearful, separative belief system, we will perceive our lives as painful and chaotic. God's contribution is the love and light that is always shining, we just can't see it.

Formal prayers are usually initiated at the point when things aren't going well. Often, the pleas are directed to *rescuing or protecting us from what we have co-created with our erroneous belief that we are nothing but a weak small ego living in a body in a hostile world.* From this position we will naturally think negative thoughts, create stress, and develop all sorts of accidents, diseases and disasters. Then, we plead with God to go around his/her laws and bail us out of whatever trouble we are in. *That is not true prayer.* That is asking a more powerful relative to bail us out of jail so we can get into trouble again. God's answer to such prayers is, *"No, I will not bail you out until you learn what a spiritual point of view really is. When you experience my peace, love and light, you will pray differently and you will see the responses clearly."*

This book is an appeal to become aware of our fearful, ego centered "prayers" and make them real prayers. As we evolve, spiritually, it is only natural to bring our thoughts and feelings into line with God's will. This book is a tool that can be utilized to develop such a keen awareness of our deepest nature that our lives become a prayer, a prayer to live our lives in a Godly way, rather than the ego oriented way, protecting ourselves from fear and guilt.

Through my own prayers and studying transpersonal psychology, including *A Course In Miracles* (Christian), Kabbalah (Jewish), Jane Roberts (New Age), Buddhism, Vedanta Hinduism, and others, it is clear to me that our true nature is *love*. The purpose of prayer is to remove any and all blocks to our loving nature. The biggest block to love is fear, fear of physical harm, fear of psychological harm, fear of our own feelings. Prayer helps us overcome fear through faith, opening us up to love. When we say our lives have become a prayer, it means our faith is so strong that fear is dissipated. This leaves us free to feel and manifest our compassionate love.

Most of us spend too much time in externally oriented pursuits. The ego wants us to have this distracted form of awareness because it doesn't know who we really are. Prayer helps us by bringing us closer to unifying the ego with the Ground of Being. It is very difficult to get the ego to acknowledge its inevitable alliance with God, but it is necessary and can be accomplished in different ways by the various forms of prayer. The practical effects of the ego allying with the Ground (God) are many including, calmness, kindness, alertness, happiness and compassion. In other words, allying and unifying the ego and the Ground (God) removes fear and reveals our loving nature.

The goal of prayer is Self realization. With Self realization comes God realization. Prayer helps us harmonize our will with God's will, through the removal of fear, guilt, hate and inferiority. None of this can be accomplished, however, while under the externally oriented melodrama of the ego. The ego constantly tells us that we must be afraid or we will be annihilated. Thus, according to the ego, it is good to be afraid because our fears protects us. In reality it is not good or necessary to be afraid. Prayer helps us to see that the ego gives us an incomplete and erroneous perception of our true nature. Prayer reveals to us that we are much more than we think we are. Prayer removes the cloak of fear that the ego likes to keep drawn over our true loving nature.

No behavioral or psychoanalytic talk therapy can help us to develop a spiritual point of view, since there is no spiritual element in these therapies. Behavioral therapy sees human beings as complex machines. If they break they can be "fixed" by counter conditioning or behavior modification. Psychoanalytic therapy goes deeper than behaviorism in recognizing that there is an unconscious. However, the unconscious is seen only as a hotbed of repressed emotions and sexual and aggressive drives. Though it is helpful to recognize, feel and process our projected, denied and repressed emotions, the healing is incomplete. Fear still rules us. No Spiritual element is accessed or acknowledged. The best outcome of psychoanalytic therapy is a stronger ego to fight against an alleged hostile physical world that we should be afraid of.

Existential therapy takes the hostile world theory to its logical conclusion. Existentialists tell us that, since we are merely finite, physical creatures, we are naturally afraid of death and fear taking responsibility for our free choices in this, our one and only chance at life. At the end, say the existentialists, we will just disappear into oblivion anyway. Their solution is basically to "suck it up": admit that we are separate finite creatures, face the inevitable fear and take responsibility for a very limited but potentially meaningful life. Existential philosophy itself is limited because it doesn't develop our faith in a Higher Power.

Spiritual or transpersonal therapy has the potential for true healing because it assumes that we are spiritual beings who have temporarily taken physical form. John Mundy, who writes about the Course in Miracles in his book *Listening To Your Inner Guide*, talks about his own near-death experience, which convinced him that he is primarily a spiritual being. During his near-death experience, he felt his consciousness surviving his body. Thus, he *knows* that the body is the temporary delusion and that only spirit is real. Like most near-death survivors, Mundy feels his experience was beyond words. Yet, it was so powerful that this knowledge led him to *A Course In Miracles* idea that we, in the physical world, have everything backwards. It is our Spiritual consciousness that *creates this illusion* we call physical reality. Acceptance of even this one idea would go far towards eliminating anxiety.

Jane Roberts' Seth Material

This same idea is echoed in the earlier mentioned Seth philosophy of Jane Roberts. Roberts tells us that physical reality is created from the dream state. It is then filtered through our conscious and unconscious beliefs and the result is our physical world. Mass events are also created this way through mass consciousness, emotion and belief.

I recall two examples of mass consciousness creating a physical event, the weather. When the Iranian hostages came home to Lake Placid, New York, the temperature was at least 30 degrees higher than normal. Truly, they received a warm welcome home, on what could have ordinarily been a cold winter's day. The second event was an unusual snow squall that blew through New York during John Lennon's public funeral in Central Park. This matched the anguish of the grievers for Lennon.

What If Mass Consciousness Became Spiritual

Maharishi Mahesh Yogi had a beautiful dream. He felt that if enough people practiced TM, world peace would be the result. This later became known as the "Maharishi Effect." This effect, if verified, would follow the Jane Roberts' teaching that mass consciousness creates physical reality. As long as most of the people believe that they are primarily bodies, directed by egos, there will be fear, guilt, hate and inferiority. At a mass level there will be war, famine, weather and earth change disasters, and epidemics. Most predictions of global disasters at the Millennium are based upon the hysteria created by masses of fearful, ego-centered, emotionally charged people. However, if enough people, pray, meditate and shift their locus of thought to Spiritual consciousness, a very different future is in store for the Earth and it's inhabitants. This Maharishi effect would be manifested throughout the world.

Philosopher Michael Grosso points out the importance of a paradigm shift from fear to spirituality, in his book, *The Millennium Myth*. Grosso feels that there is still time to change our way of thinking. Such change will produce a different, more positive experience of the Millennium than most seers have imagined. Futurist Willis Harman, in his book *Global Mind Change*, concurs with Grosso. He states,

"Because of the interconnectedness of all minds with the universal mind, we can be sure that the tasks to which we are directed will be most effective in solving the world's fundamental illness, of which hunger and poverty and plague and pestilence and war are all a part. We need not fear that in pursuing our own real self interest we will fail to contribute maximally to the real self interest of others." (Harman, 1988, p 168) This is true if we begin to consciously manifest our true Self, with a Spiritual or transpersonal orientation. By turning to God in prayer, we can create and perceive more "win-win" situations. If enough people can develop the transpersonal orientation, world peace will be created.

Start Where You Are

Each of us can only start where we are. Even if we are totally ego driven, we must realize that if we want peace of mind we *must* go outside the ego system to get it. Prayer of any type referred to in this book is just such a turning toward God. Determine what your primary problems are and earnestly begin to pray in whatever way seems best. Using the suggested materials in this book, write you own affirmative prayers, aiming toward faith, love, forgiveness and strength. Pray for guidance in making Spiritually sensitive life decisions. Pray for the ability to see situations anew, creating win-win solutions to your challenges. Pray for a Spiritual mind shift to heal friends, relatives and all beings in Spirit, mind and body. Pray with adoration of the awe inspiring grandeur of God or the Ground of Being. Meditate with an open mind for insight into your true nature. Meditate with single minded devotion on your mantra. It will lead to your experiencing the oneness of all creation.

Persist in your prayers and meditations. Observe the betterment of your life as you shift from the ego to the Higher Self in your orientation to the world. Be aware that gradually, your life is becoming a prayer, a prayer that is answered as all prayers are. But now, as you pray from the Godly point of view, you will see more clearly how your prayers are answered. As ever more and more people shift to the transpersonal point of view, the outer world will become transformed in ways we can only glimpse now. By praying daily from the heart, you are doing your part in transforming the world, as well as the cosmos. *Namaste, Shalom, peace* be with you.

Appendix A

Suggestions On Praying Psychologically

- Make a commitment to yourself to pray daily.

- Choose a convenient time and commit to it. Morning prayer sets a good tone for the day.

- Ask those living with you not to interrupt. Fifteen to twenty minutes should be enough.

- Take a few minutes to get centered and relaxed. You may want to count your breaths from one to four several times.

- Pray from the heart. You may use thoughts or images that make you feel thankful, peaceful and loving.

- Make your prayers affirmative. For example; I am perfect, whole, happy and healthy.

- Make your prayers thankful. For example; Thank you God for bringing love, peace and abundance into my life.

- Pray for the strength and guidance to make positive character growth. This counters inferiority feelings.

- Pray for an increase in faith. This counters basic fear.

- Pray for forgiveness of self and others. This counters guilt.

- Pray for unconditional love of self and others. This counters hate of self (for imperfection) and others.

- Pray for the enlightenment of all people.

- Be careful what you pray for. Your prayers will be answered in some way, though it may not be the way you think.

- Pray for the replacement of negative, limiting beliefs by positive beliefs. Be specific.

- Pray for the ability to take appropriate action to reach your goals.

- Ask for guidance via questions to God or the "higher power."

- Listen for answers. Thank God for the guidance.

APPENDIX B

UNDERLYING ASSUMPTIONS OF HEALING THROUGH PRAYER

- All Minds are joined.

- At the deepest level, we are all One.

- This oneness enables us to influence each other according to our intent.

- This influence may be positive or negative.

- We are here on Earth to learn to focus our intent in a positive loving manner-there is nothing else for us to do.

- Focusing our love will help others to the extent they are open to it.

- God exists-all is God.

- God is love-we have the God spark within-therefore we are love also.

- As we become aware of our God spark within, we draw closer to God and are able to feel more peaceful and loving.

- We can heal ourselves and others by drawing closer to God through meditation and prayer.

- We can learn to meditate and pray more effectively.

- There are spiritual and psychological issues behind every physical illness.

- We can foster our own growth through accepting our lives, allowing our experiences and learning from them-this is the "allow" state.

- We need to "process" our emotional blockages to spiritual growth-caused by hurt, disappointment and trauma-before we can release the anger, fear and guilt that make us unhappy.

- Each time we "process" and "release" a painful feeling we raise our vibratory level, moving to a higher, more responsible, more spiritual state.

- The processing and releasing of painful emotions leads us to our core beliefs. These core beliefs have been learned through many lifetimes.

- If we go through enough releases of painful emotions, newer more peaceful, loving, spiritual beliefs emerge to take the place of the old dysfunctional core beliefs.

- Core beliefs are held in place physically, it seems like letting go of them and changing them will result in our death and complete obliteration, thus there is much resistance to changing them.

REFERENCES

Introduction

Freud, Anna, *The Ego And Mechanisms Of Defense*, Rev. Ed., New York, International Universities Press, 1967.

Freud Sigmund, *Basic Works of Sigmund Freud*, Franklin Center Pa., Franklin Library, 1978.

Kushner, Harold, *When Bad Things Happen To Good People*, New York, Shocken Books, 1981.

Chapter One

Assagioli, Roberto, *Psychosynthesis*, New York, Viking Press, 1965.

Goldsmith, Joel, *The Art Of Spiritual Healing*, New York, Harper Collins, 1959.

Roberts, Jane, *The Nature Of Personal Reality*, Englewood Cliffs, N.J. Prentice-Hall, 1974.

Chapter Two

Beck, Aaron, *The Cognitive Therapy of Depression*, New York, Guilford Press, 1979.

Guidano and Liotti, *Cognitive Therapy of Emotional Disorders*, New York, Academic Press, 1983.

Holmes, Ernest, *The Science of Mind*, New York, Dodd, Mead and Co., 1938.

Chapter Three

Goldsmith, Joel, *Collected Essays of Joel Goldsmith*, Marina Del Rey Ca., De Vorss and Co., 1986.

Holmes, Ernest, *The Science of Mind*, New York, Dodd, Mead and Co., 1938.

Jung, C.G., *The Basic Writings of C.G. Jung*, New York, Modern Library, 1959.

Levine, Stephen, *A Gradual Awakening*, Garden City, N.Y., Anchor Press:Doubleday, 1979.

Roberts, Jane, *The Nature of Personal Reality*, Englewood Cliffs N.J., Prentice Hall, 1974.

Washburn, Michael, *The Ego and the Dynamic Ground*, Albany, N.Y., SUNY Press, 1988.

Chapter Four

Horney, Karen, *Neurosis and Human Growth*, New York, W.W. Norton, 1950.

Miller, Alice, *The Drama of the Gifted Child*, New York, Basic Books, 1981.

Pierrakos, Eva, and Thesenga, Donovan, *Surrender to God Within, Pathwork at the Soul Level*, Del Mar Ca., Pathwork Press, 1997.

Washburn, Michael, *The Ego and the Dynamic Ground*, Albany N.Y., SUNY Press, 1988.

Weekes, Claire, *Hope and Help For Your Nerves*, New York, Hawthorne Books, 1969.

Wilber, Ken, *The Spectrum of Consciousness in Transformation of Consciousness*, Boston, Shambalha, 1986, pp. 65-126.

Chapter Five

Assagioli, Roberto, *Psychosynthesis,* New York, Viking Press, 1965.

Becker, Ernest, *The Denial of Death, Man's Transformation of Reality*, New York, Free Press, 1973.

Erickson, Milton, and Rossi, Ernest, *The Collected Papers of Milton Erickson*, New York, Irvington, 1980.

Frankl, Victor, *Man's Search for Ultimate Meaning*, New York, Insight Books, 1997.

Jung, C.G. *The Basic Writings of C.G. Jung*, New York, Modern Library, 1859.

Chapter Six

A Course in Miracles, Tiburon, Ca., Foundation For Inner Peace, 1975.

Dyer, Wayne, *Your Sacred Self*, New York, Harper, 1997.

Spangler, David, *Everyday Miracles: The Inner Art of Manifestation*, New York, Bantam, 1996.

Washburn, Michael, *Transpersonal Psychology in Psychoanalytic Perspective*, Albany N.Y., SUNY Press, 1994.

Chapter Seven

A Course in Miracles, Tiburon, Ca., Foundation For Inner Peace, 1975.

Casarjian, Robin, *Forgiveness: A Bold Choice for a Peaceful Heart*, New York, Bantam, 1992.

Ferrucci, Piero, *What We May Be*, Los Angeles, J.P. Tarcher, 1981.

Jung, C.G., *The Basic Writings of C.G. Jung,* New York, Modern Library, 1959.

Miller, Alice, *Breaking Down The Wall of Silence*, New York, Penguin, 1991.

Miller, Carolyn, *Creating Miracles: Understanding the Experience of Divine Intervention*, Tiburon, Ca., H,J, Kramer, 1995.

Chapter Eight

Hubert, Sandra, *Your Soul Can Heal You*, Unpublished Manuscript.

Jung, C.G. *The Basic Writings of C.G. Jung,* New York, Modern Library, 1959.

Chapter Nine

A Course in Miracles, Tiburon, Ca., Foundation For Inner Peace, 1975.

Bailes, Frederick, *Hidden Power for Human Problems*, Englewood Cliffs, N.J., Prentice Hall, 1957.

Groddek, George, *The Meaning of Illness*, New York, International Universities Press, 1997.

Sacerdote, Paul, "Hypnotically Elicited Mystical States in Treating Physical and Emotional Pain", in Hammond, Cory, *Handbook of Hypnotic Suggestions and Metaphors*, New York, W.W. Norton, 1990.

Chapter Ten

Assagioli, Roberto, *Psychosynthesis*, Viking Press, New York, 1965.

Dyer, Wayne, *Your Sacred Self*, New York, Harper, 1997.

Erickson, M., and Rossi, E, *The Collected Papers of Milton Erickson*, New York, Irvington, 1980.

Fox, Emmet, *Stake Your Claim*, New York, Harper, 1952.

Frankl, Victor, *Man's Search for Ultimate Meaning*, New York, Insight Books, 1997.

Gurdjieff, George, *Gurdjieff: Essays and Reflections On the Man and His Teaching*, New York, Continuum, 1995.

Kierkegaard, Soren, *Either/Or* Princeton N.J., Princeton University Press, 1987.

Nietzsche, Friedreich, *Beyond Good and Evil*, Buffalo, N.Y., Prometheus Books, 1989.

Sartre, Jean Paul, *Nausea*, New York, New Directions, 1964.

Tillich, Paul, *The Courage To Be*, New Haven CT., Yale University Press, 1952.

Yalom, Irwin, *Existential Psychotherapy*, New York, Basic Books, 1980.

Chapter Eleven

Dossey, Larry, *Healing Words, The Power of Prayer: The Practice of Medicine*, New York, Harper Collins, 1993.

Dossey, Larry, *Prayer Is Good Medicine*, San Francisco, Ca., Harper Collins, 1996.

Dossey, Larry, *Be Careful What You Pray For, You Just Might Get It, What We Can Do About the Unintentional Effects of Our Prayers*, San Francisco, Harper Collins, 1997.

Erickson, Milton and Rossi, Ernest, *The Collected Papers of Milton H. Erickson*, New York, Irvington, 1980.

Hudson, Thompson J., *The Law of Psychic Phenomena: A Working Hypothesis for the Systematic Study of Hypnotism, Spiritism , Mental Therapeutics Etc.*, Chicago, A.C. Mc Clurg, 1893.

Chapter Twelve

Bucke, R.M., *Cosmic Consciousness: A Study in the Evolution of the Human Mind*, New York, E.P. Dutton, 1996.

Freeman, Arthur, *"Spirituality, Well Being and Ministry"*, in *Journal of Pastoral Care*, Spring, 1998, Vol. 52, No. 1, pp. 7-17.

Horney, Karen, *Neurosis and Human Growth*, New York, W.W. Norton, 1950.

Huxley, Aldous, *The Perennial Philosophy*, New York, Harper and Row, 1944.

Chapter Thirteen

A Course in Miracles, Tiburon, Ca., Foundation For Inner Peace, 1975.

Benson, Herbert, *The Relaxation Response*, New York, Morrow, 1975.

Benson, Herbert, *Beyond the Relaxation Response: How to Harness the Healing Power of Your Personal Beliefs*, New York, Times Books, 1984.

Benson, Herbert, *Timeless Healing*, New York, Scribner, 1996.

Carrington, Patricia, *Freedom in Meditation*, Garden City, New York, Anchor Press, Doubleday, 1977.

Humphreys, Christmas, *Concentration and Meditation*, Rockport, Ma., Element, 1968.

Kabat-Zinn, Jon, *Full Catastrophe Living*, New York, Bantam, 1990.

Kabat-Zinn, Jon, *Wherever You Go, There You Are*, New York, Hyperion, 1994.

Kornfield, Jack, *A Path With Heart: A Guide Through the Perils and Promise of Spiritual Life*, New York, Bantam, 1993.

Leichtman R. and Japiske C., *Active Meditation*, Columbus, Ohio, Ariel Press, 1980.

Le Shan, Lawrence, *How To Meditate*, New York, Bantam, 1974.

Levine, Stephen, *A Gradual Awakening*, Garden City, N.Y., Anchor Press, Doubleday, 1979.

Mundy, Jon, *Listening To Your Inner Guide*, New York, Crossroad, 1995.

Roberts, Jane, *The Nature of Personal Reality*, Englewood cliffs, N.J., Prentice-Hall, 1974.

Washburn, Michael, *The Ego and the Dynamic Ground*, Albany, N.Y., SUNY Press, 1988.

Chapter Fourteen

A Course in Miracles, Tiburon, Ca., Foundation For Inner Peace, 1975.

Mundy, Jon, *Listening to Your Inner Guide*, New York, Crossroad, 1995.

Roberts, Jane, *The Individual and the Nature of Mass Events: A Seth Book*, Englewood Cliffs N.J., Prentice-Hall, 1981.